COMMUNITY
LEADERSHIP
Through
Community-Based
Programming

COMMUNITY LEADERSHIP
Through
Community-Based Programming

The Role of the Community College

Edgar J. Boone and Associates
Academy for Community College Leadership
Advancement, Innovation, and Modeling
North Carolina State University

Foreword by David R. Pierce

Community College Press

Edgar J. Boone and Associates
Academy for Community College Leadership
Advancement, Innovation, and Modeling
North Carolina State University

**Community Leadership Through Community-Based Programming
The Role of the Community College**

Community College Press

© 1997 by the American Association of Community Colleges

Printed in the United States of America.

Published by the
Community College Press
American Association of Community Colleges
One Dupont Circle, NW, Suite 410
Washington, DC 20036
202/728-0200
http://www.aacc.nche.edu

ISBN 0-87117-302-6

Contents

Foreword

A ny book that proposes to enhance the role of the community college in renewing America's communities must balance theory with practical advice, grounded in solid research and tempered by extensive field-testing. Such a work should not simply challenge the reader to think in new ways. It must also offer sound and tested strategies that provide substantial assurance of improving a community's quality of life. *Community Leadership Through Community-Based Programming: The Role of the Community College* does both.

In this important new work, Edgar Boone, George Vaughan, and their colleagues at North Carolina State University describe a process—the ACCLAIM process—that has a proven track record of empowering community colleges to engage their communities in more efficient and effective ways. The success of this process derives in large measure from its strong theoretical base and its well-developed implementation strategy. ACCLAIM begins with the conviction that community colleges are community-based institutions, devoted to improving the quality of life of the citizens and communities they serve. To this conviction, the ACCLAIM process marries a well-defined program that facilitates greater collaboration among community-based organizations, formal and informal leaders, and citizens in pursuit of this vital goal.

Community Leadership Through Community-Based Programming: The Role of the Community College comes at an especially opportune moment. Increasingly, community college leaders recognize that the challenges in the 21st century cannot be met within the boundaries of traditional degree programs and on-campus instruction. Although venturing beyond these boundaries is nothing new for many community colleges, the challenges of the next century will differ from those of the past in kind, not merely in degree. This book offers a blueprint equal to the demands of this new era, through which community college leaders can join with the people, their leaders, and other community organizations to seek out, identify, and resolve threats to the quality of community life.

I urge my colleagues in community colleges, in state agencies, and in community-based organizations to look closely at the ACCLAIM process as a model for the future, offering communities a vital new avenue to renewal and revitalization.

David R. Pierce, President
American Association of
Community Colleges
January 1997

Preface

Community Leadership Through Community-Based Programming: The Role of the Community College gives practical, field-tested guidance on successfully applying the concepts and principles of community-based programming in today's community college. This new work is based on the extensive experience of the Academy for Community College Leadership Advancement, Innovation, and Modeling (ACCLAIM) in helping community colleges effectively implement community-based programming in their service area communities.

This work is not a textbook nor is it intended for the exclusive use of community college educators. The concepts, principles, and methods presented are applicable to all adult education organizations and community-based institutions that have an interest in and commitment to resolving issues and empowering people. The book is intended for pragmatic use by community college administrators, governing boards, and other influential community leaders interested in strengthening their community colleges, developing their communities, and serving the ends of democracy.

Community Leadership Through Community-Based Programming: The Role of the Community College contains seven chapters that define and describe the community-based programming process and strategies and techniques that can be used for its implementation.

Chapter 1 introduces and describes the community-based programming process. Community-based programming is a systematic and rational process in which the community college functions as a leader and catalyst in effecting collaboration among the people, their leaders, and community-based agencies and organizations in identifying, confronting, and resolving critical community issues that are adversely affecting—or have the potential to adversely affect—the community, its people, and their quality of life. Community-based programming includes 15 interconnected processual tasks that, if effectively implemented, can greatly aid the community college in becoming a leader and catalyst in helping the people, their leaders, and community agencies and organizations learn how to work together in a team effort to resolve community issues. The subsequent chapters describe in detail the processual tasks and suggest strategies and techniques that can be used to implement them.

Chapter 2 outlines how community colleges go about institutionalizing the community-based programming process. The first three processual tasks are addressed in that chapter. Special attention is given to the president's role in the institutionalization process. Suggestions are offered for how community colleges can institutionalize community-based programming.

Chapter 3 describes the environmental scanning process, an integral part of community-based programming. Through environmental scanning, the college can identify and begin to understand the most significant issues affecting the quality of life of citizens in the community college's service area. The process leads to selection of a single issue to be addressed by the community college in its first community-based programming effort. The chapter explains the function and organization of the environmental scanning committee and suggests who its members might be, including criteria for selecting and training community leaders and experts for membership on the committee. This chapter presents and explains processual tasks 4, 5, and 6.

Chapter 4 presents concepts and skills needed for implementing processual tasks 7, 8, 9, and 10. To implement these tasks the community college must first study, analyze, and map the target publics and stakeholders affected by the issue identified through the environmental scanning process. This is a critical point in the community-based programming process because it is at this juncture that the community college begins work on a specific issue. The concepts and skills presented in chapter 4 include identifying target public and stakeholders, applying sociological tools to mapping the publics, identifying leaders of the target public and stakeholders, involving those leaders as members of a coalition to study, analyze, and refine the definition of the issue; establishing a goal to be achieved that will result in resolution of the issue; and selecting strategies for resolving the issue and achieving the goal.

Chapter 5 describes how decisions made by a coalition formed to address an issue are translated into a plan of action. It also elaborates on the strategies that must be followed to assure that the plan of action is effectively implemented. These steps are encompassed in processual tasks 11 and 12.

Chapter 6 focuses on evaluation and accountability in community-based programming and presents approaches for implementing processual tasks 13, 14, and 15. Since the coalition's first attempt is not likely to resolve the issue totally, the coalition's efforts will usually be iterative, with improvements being made in strategies (reflected in the learner objective, learning activities, resources, and how those resources are used) with each cycle. The chapter stresses the importance of the evaluation process in measuring the success of the plan of action, reporting outcomes to stakeholders, and using lessons learned to improve the plan of action.

Chapter 7 summarizes ACCLAIM's observations and lessons learned in implementing the community-based programming process in its pilot demonstration community colleges. Based on those findings, recommendations for implementing the community-based programming process are offered to community colleges that have an interest in becoming more actively involved in the affairs of their respective service-area communities.

Sincere acknowledgment and appreciation are extended to Dr. Tom Knecht, colleague and friend, for editing the entire manuscript and considerably improving its quality and readability. Special thanks are due Robert Pedersen and the American Association of Community Colleges for publishing the book. Appreciation is expressed to Mrs. Ruth Shultz, ACCLAIM's Administrative Officer, for untiring efforts in attending to the many details associated with ACCLAIM. A debt of gratitude and thanks are extended to ACCLAIM's nine pilot demonstration community colleges that committed the leadership, resources, and time required to institutionalize and implement the community-based programming process in their respective institutions: in North Carolina, James Sprunt Community College and Guilford Technical Community College; in South Carolina, Technical College of the Lowcountry and Florence-Darlington Technical Community College; in Virginia, Paul D. Camp Community College, Southside Virginia Community College, Blue Ridge Community College, and Thomas Nelson Community College; and in Maryland, Charles County Community College.

Special gratitude is expressed to the W. K. Kellogg Foundation, North Carolina State University, and the North Carolina, South Carolina, Virginia, and Maryland Community College Systems for the financial resources provided ACCLAIM. Without the generous financial support provided by these parties, the community-based programming project would have remained a vision rather than the reality it is today. Deserving of particular recognition are the W. K. Kellogg Foundation's Dr. Russell G. Mawby, CEO Emeritus, Dr. Norman A. Brown, President Emeritus, Dr. Valora Washington, Vice President, and Dr. Tyrone R. Baines, Program Leader, who together provided the support and continuing encouragement that has enabled ACCLAIM to bring renewal to the lives of individuals and of entire communities through the strategies described in this work.

Edgar J. Boone, Director
ACCLAIM

An Introduction to the Community-Based Programming Process

1

A merica is at a critical juncture in its history as it prepares for the twenty-first century. From its inception as a nation committed to democracy, America has consistently turned to its people for renewal and for a reaffirmation of those basic values essential to the maintenance of a strong, dynamic, and open society. America continues to be a nation of, for, and governed by the people.

During the last half of the twentieth century, however, America has witnessed a rapid erosion of the democratic precepts held by its people. Indeed, Americans have increasingly looked to the government to confront and solve their problems, and this form of dependency has become a norm that permeates every aspect of their lives. This trend toward dependency is manifest in an alarming deterioration in the quality of life characterized by a sense of hopelessness and powerlessness and by lack of initiative, self-sufficiency, and resolve. Out of this milieu, problems and issues have emerged that threaten the very fabric of American democracy. Underemployment and unemployment; adult illiteracy; polluted environments; failing school systems; increasing crime; rising substance abuse; concern over health services; and ethnic tensions can only be resolved by a people that embrace a spirit of collaboration and develop a sense of community in which they can use to the full potential their rich personal talent and considerable resources.

The need in America is to renew and rebuild the concept of community, in which people are empowered and provided the opportunity to develop their innate leadership abilities within their own surroundings.

The rebirth of the American community entails restoring among the people a sense of identity and belonging, of opportunity for allegiance, of being needed and of responding to needs. This challenge can be met and resolved. The question is: How can a sense of community be restored? Currently, the American community is at a crossroads in seeking a process through which to stimulate, motivate, and empower its people and their leaders to work together to collectively identify, study, and analyze issues affecting their well-being and quality of life and to mount programs leading to resolution of these issues. Although there are numerous publicly and privately supported community-based agencies and organizations, most have specialized functions and serve narrowly defined publics and agendas. These agencies and organizations respond to the particular needs of their constituents, but their programmatic efforts are often fragmented and lack continuity, making it impossible for any of them alone to address broad issues of public concern. They do, however, have resources and expertise that, if skillfully combined with those of other community agencies and organizations in a team effort involving the people of the community, could have a measurable impact on community issues and greatly aid in the empowerment of people.

There is a need to create in the community a forum for its people and community agencies and organizations to collaborate in team efforts to confront and resolve those issues that are critical to the community and the well-being of its people. A concomitant and most desirable consequence of such an environment is the empowerment of people and the development of local leadership to take control of their own destinies. To reestablish this sense of community and create a nurturing environment, there is a need for a community leader and catalyst to galvanize the people and community agencies and organizations into collaborative action.

The Community College as Leader and Catalyst

From its founding as a people's college, the community college has had the potential to function in a leader-catalyst role in its community and to provide the initiative, motivation, and nurturance to rally and sustain the people, their leaders, and other community agencies and organizations in collaborative decision-making focusing on the identification and resolution of the most important community issues. As an open-door institution committed to serving the educational needs of the people in its community, the community college is ideally situated to function as a leader-catalyst in bringing people and leaders of other community agencies and organizations together in a collaborative spirit.

Several factors provide a strong case for the community college to assume this role as leader and catalyst:

1. The community college is embedded in the fabric of its community by virtue of its founding legislation, mission, funding base and achievements.
2. The comprehensiveness that characterizes the programs and resources of the community college is a strength unequalled by most community agencies and organizations.
3. The public has a positive perception of the community college's capability, and there is a strong bond between the community college and its community.
4. The community college is viewed by the people and other community agencies and organizations as a neutral institution devoted to education.
5. The community college has extensive knowledge of and sensitivity to the social, economic, technological, and political forces that shape the environment of its community.

How does the community college position itself to perform as a leader and catalyst in effecting collaboration among the people, their leaders, and other community agencies and organizations in its community in identifying and resolving critical issues that affect the quality of life of the people? The answer lies in a process we call *community-based programming.*

Community-based programming is a process involving a series of interconnected *processual tasks* in which the community college functions as a leader and catalyst in effecting collaboration among the people, their leaders, and other community agencies and organizations in identifying and seeking resolution of major community issues. The concept of processual task is central to the meaning of this work. This concept was developed by the author some years ago to lift adult educators' thinking to a conceptual level in which programmatic situations are viewed from a process orientation, rather than from a mechanistic perspective. Some approaches to adult education have prescribed rules-based steps that, if mechanically followed, are expected to produce the desired outcomes. In practice, only relatively simple adult education programs can be successfully developed on the basis of prescribed rules. Programs designed to bring about a change in fundamental behaviors or to address and resolve broad social issues require a more flexible, conceptual approach based on systems thinking. Implementing a processual task requires devising and carrying out a complex set of actions tailored to the individual situation. Essential to the successful completion of a processual task is the definition of the intended outcome and selection and implementation of conceptually-driven actions leading to achievement of that outcome.

Embodied within this definition are several concepts, including catalyst, issue, collaboration, and coalition.

In the community-based programming process, the community college is defined as the catalyst in its community for initiating and facilitating collaboration among the people, their leaders, and other community agencies and organizations in identifying and resolving critical issues that are affecting the quality of life of the community and its people. As a catalyst, the community college works (1) to focus the attention of the people, their leaders, and other community agencies and organizations on identifying and prioritizing the issues that affect the quality of life of people and their community; (2) to stimulate and motivate the people, their leaders, and other community agencies and organizations to work together to analyze a specified issue and reach consensus on a collaborative plan for its resolution; and (3) to provide continuing care and nurturance to the team effort needed to implement the plan and assess its impact on resolving the issue.

Community-based programming is issue-driven. An issue is defined as a matter of wide public concern that influences the daily lives of people. Issues have three key features: (1) they exist in the broad dimensions of the entire society; (2) they have their source in complex and interrelated problems—economic, social, political, and technological—that are characterized by divergent viewpoints, shifting public perceptions, and conflicting values in an age of instability; and (3) they frequently involve conflict and controversy that require mediation of disputes among competing interests.

Community-based programming involves collaboration and coalition building. To collaborate in community-based programming is to work with others in identifying, analyzing, and seeking solutions to an issue. Implicit in collaboration is the mutual agreement by those involved on the definition of the issue, the goal to be pursued and a plan of action. And collaboration among the people directly affected by the issue and the community agencies and organizations that have a stake in the issue ideally leads to the formation of a coalition of their leaders and representatives. A coalition is a temporary association of individuals and groups that have a common interest in and commitment to the resolution of an issue. The coalition combines human and material resources to seek a resolution of the issue in a manner that would be beyond the capacity of any one group or organization acting alone. Coalitions formed and used in the community-based programming process are composed of leaders representing the target public and key stakeholders, those who are affected by or have a stake in a defined issue **A coalition increases the critical mass that can be brought to bear to resolve any issue.**

The Community-Based Programming Process

Community-based programming involves clearly defined, orderly, processual tasks that, when fully implemented, result in predictable outcomes. The outcomes sought are (1) the identification of and movement toward the resolution of major issues that are important to the community and its people; (2) the creation of a unified force that transcends the forces of fragmentation in the community and cultivates a spirit of teamwork, resolution, and optimism within the people, their leaders, and stakeholder groups and organizations; (3) the acceptance of high community expectations by all parties as a result of working together and developing a broad-based, community system to deal with current and future issues of wide public concern; and (4) the emergence and development of broadly representative leaders. To achieve these outcomes, the following sequence of processual tasks is suggested for community colleges to use in their approach to community-based programming.

Processual Task 1. The community college develops and adopts a definition of community-based programming that encompasses those basic principles and concepts required to fulfill its mission as a community-based institution.

Recognizing that each community college has a unique culture, serves a unique community, and is ultimately governed by its mission, there are, nonetheless, certain basic tenets that the community college needs to follow if it is to function as a community-based institution. Once members of the college community understand and accept these basic tenets, it is important that the governing board, community leaders, and others associated with the community college also understand, accept, and be committed to this definition.

In developing its definition of community-based programming, the community college needs to take into consideration the social, economic, technological, and political forces that shape the institution and its community. Processual task 1 is the first step in aiding the community college in fulfilling its mission as a community-based institution. It provides the foundation for all other tasks in the community-based programming process.

> **Processual Task 2.** The community college engages in a careful study of its community to increase its knowledge of its social-cultural, economic, technological, and political environment.

The community college's success in community-based programming will depend, in large measure, on its leaders' and staff's knowledge of the environment in which the college functions. The president, senior administrators, and staff need to know about those local, regional, state, and national forces that are interactive and are influencing the options open to the people in the college's service area. An understanding of the college's service area and how it is linked to the larger environment is a prerequisite to the community college's involvement in community-based programming. It is within this informed context that the community college initiates and engages in community-based programming.

> **Processual Task 3.** The community college examines and, if needed, reinterprets or modifies its mission, philosophy, goals, organizational structure, and mode of operation to emphasize community-based programming as one of its major programmatic efforts.

The college's decision to infuse community-based programming through its mission lays the foundation for positioning the college to serve as a leader and catalyst in effecting collaboration among all community elements in addressing critical issues. As a result, the community college may need to reposition itself to fulfill its potential as a leader and catalyst in its community. Such repositioning will, in most instances, require that the community college reinterpret or modify its mission and re-examine its goals to emphasize community-based programming. Further, the philosophy that the institution embraces and that currently guides the behavior of its staff will need to accentuate those beliefs and values that will inspire the college's involvement in the affairs of its community.

The organizational structure and resources of the college may need to be realigned so that it can effectively practice community-based programming. The extent to which a community college becomes committed to and involved in community-based programming will depend, in large measure, upon the processes through which the resources it will need for community-based programming are identified, attained, utilized, and managed. Of special importance to community-based programming are the community college's management practices; they should facilitate its staff's commitment to and involvement in community-based programming. In addition, the community college leaders must make a concerted effort to involve the staff, the faculty, and governing board in the repositioning of the college to strengthen broad ownership in this effort.

To guide and facilitate its involvement in community-based programming, the community college will need to establish a community-based programming management team that is an integral part of the president's office. Generally, the president does not serve on the management team. The multiple responsibilities associated with the president's leadership position does not allow him or her sufficient flexibility to devote the time and energy needed to handle the intensive and continuing attention and work that will be required for the management team in facilitating the college's implementation of community-based programming. Members of the management team serve in an ex-officio capacity to the environmental scanning committee.

Specific functions of the community-based programming management team include:

■ assisting the president in forming an environmental scanning committee and engaging it in continuous scanning of the college's external environment;

■ managing the college's efforts to study, analyze, and map the target
publics and stakeholders specific to issues;

■ engaging leaders of the target publics and stakeholders in an analysis
of the issue;

■ forming an issue-specific coalition made up of the leaders of the target public and stakeholders;

■ guiding the coalition in its deliberations and in designing and implementing a plan of action aimed at resolving the issue; and

■ assisting the coalition to assess the outcomes achieved from implementing the plan of action and assessing the community college's
community-based programming efforts as a whole.

While the core of the management team's membership is constant, its
work on a specific issue will be greatly strengthened through the *ad hoc*
involvement of additional members of the community college's staff and
community leaders who are knowledgeable about the issue, its target public, and stakeholders. For example, with respect to an issue that focuses on
adult literacy, community leaders who are knowledgeable about adult illiteracy in the college's service area would be invaluable in helping the management team map the target public and stakeholders and in identifying and
engaging their leaders in analyzing and defining the issue.

Critical to the community college's institutionalization and effective
implementation of the community-based programming process is the
socialization of its administrators, faculty, governing officials, and key
community leaders to the process through an on-going staff development
program. Effective implementation of each processual task requires that
these community college staff groups and leaders become knowledgeable
about community-based programming skills and proficient in their use. It is
particularly important that the members of the community college's community-based programming management team become experts in the community-based programming process so that they will be able to teach the
process and facilitate and guide the community college in its implementation. Thus, the community college will need to develop and maintain an

ongoing staff development program that focuses on the community-based programming process, and the skills needed to implement it.

> **Processual Task 4.** *The community college's president establishes and employs an appropriate mechanism for scanning the college's external environment for the purposes of identifying and ranking, in order of importance, issues that are of critical concern to the community and its people.*

Community colleges must engage in environmental scanning to remain informed on both current and anticipated community issues that influence the quality of life of the people in the college's service area community. Environmental scanning first focuses on highly visible issues that are derived from the media, published reports, discussions with people, and personal observations. Trends and other data are examined and analyzed to determine whether issues are of sufficient concern to people in the service area to warrant concerted attention and action. Environmental scanning also requires that issues be ranked in priority according to their potential impact on the community.

To perform these tasks, the college will need to establish an environmental scanning committee. Ideally, its membership should include 12–15 community leaders who are knowledgeable about the community and who are willing to commit to and work with the college in its quest to become informed about the major issues confronting the community and its people. Ideally, the membership should be constant, with the team chaired by a member of the president's administrative council. Ideally, its membership would include between 12 and 15 community leaders who are willing to commit to and work with the college in its quest to become informed about major issues confronting the community and its people. Community leaders selected to serve on the environmental scanning committee might include: 1) representatives of the media; 2) economic development leaders; 3) chamber of commerce officials; 4) planning commission representatives; 5) educators; 6) cooperative extension agents; 7) elected government officials; and 8) other community leaders who are futurists. The committee scans and monitors the social, cultural, economic, technological, and political environments to produce regular "weather reports" for the college and community.

> **Processual Task 5.** *The environmental scanning committee conducts a study of the community under the leadership of the community college president.*

The community college president plays the leading role in creating the climate in which the institution's environmental scanning committee functions. The president's and the college's community-based programming management team's initial task is to organize and prepare the committee to engage in community-based programming. The committee will need guidance and support in understanding its responsibility to identify, study, and analyze community issues that are of critical concern to the community. Environmental scanning requires sampling public opinion, reading, listening to news reports, discussing concerns with community leaders and others, and examining other sources so that committee members will become well informed about the state of affairs in the community. The president, with the aid of the community-based programming management team, must provide the technical assistance and the coaching needed to aid the environmental scanning committee in obtaining and interpreting the facts surrounding the issues.

After the environmental scanning committee has identified the major issues, the group should arrive at a consensus on the ranking of the issues in terms of their relative importance to the community's welfare. While several criteria may be used in establishing the ranking, the most important criterion should focus on the severity of each issue in terms of its effect on the quality of life. The ranked issues then become the public agenda of the community. The environmental scanning committee does not disband at this juncture. Although individual members may rotate, the environmental scanning committee should become a permanent and active part of the community college's work as a leader and catalyst in facilitating positive change among the people and the community.

> **Processual Task 6.** *The community college's president seeks further confirmation and legitimation of the ranked issues from the college's governing board and from other community leaders.*

The broad-based analysis of public opinion and factual information about the community may meet all the standards of objectivity and empirical measurement, but to avoid any misconceptions or undue opposition, it is imperative that traditional sources of influence and, more particularly, the community college's governing board be consulted. These leaders should not only be kept apprised of the ongoing community-based programming effort but should also be viewed as a source of verification and legitimation. In some instances, the community college's governing board and other community leaders may be approached as a group. In others, they may be approached individually. In any event, they should not be bypassed since the potential influence of such leaders can be either a stumbling block or a stepping stone for the college in implementing the community-based programming process.

Processual Task 7. The community college studies, analyzes, and maps the public in its service area that is affected by the issue selected for resolution.

The target public is that aggregate of people who are or will be affected directly by the issue. For each issue there is a distinct target public that is, in turn, linked to other publics, referred to as stakeholders, who have or may have a vested interest in the issue and its target public. Mapping is a process of identifying how the target public is organized and functions as a social group. It also provides an understanding of the organization of stakeholder groups. Using adult illiteracy as an example, the target public consists of those adults who are defined as functionally illiterate. The stakeholder groups would likely include the school system, employers, social service agencies, public health agencies, elected governing officials, public and private adult literacy provider groups, religious organizations, and other benevolent groups.

The task is to study, analyze, and map both the target public and the stakeholder groups that have a vested interest in the issue and its target public. Many of the stakeholder groups may have programs that focus on the issue and the target public. The need is to use the appropriate conceptual tools and strategies to map and identify the groups that will be involved in developing a program to cause positive movement toward eliminating illiteracy among the service area's adult population. The process of identifying and mapping the target public and stakeholder groups would be repeated for each of the other ranked issues.

> **Processual Task 8.** *The community college selects and uses effective processes and techniques for identifying both the formal and the informal leaders within the target public and stakeholder groups.*

While mapping of the target public directly affected by the issue is critical, the key to accessing and involving that public in resolving the issue depends upon the commitment and support of its formal and informal leaders. The leaders of the target public are influential people. The goal is to identify those leaders who reflect the beliefs and values of the target public, who can speak authoritatively for members of the target public, and who can inspire the participation of the target public in working toward resolution of the issue.

Various approaches can be used to identify leaders. The more common leadership approaches are the reputational, positional, personal influence, social participation, and decision-making approaches. Which approach one adopts will vary from issue to issue, although experience suggests that a combination of leadership identification approaches may produce the best results. Again consider the illiteracy issue. In seeking funds to support a literacy program, it may be essential to seek the support of formal leaders (positional approach). But it is also crucial that the community college link with informal leaders of the target public who can help articulate their needs and secure their participation in programs designed to eliminate illiteracy (reputational and personal influence approaches). In this case, relying exclusively upon the positional approach would accomplish only part of the task of involving the target public in the literacy program.

Paralleling the need to identify leaders of the target public is the need to identify, communicate with, and establish stronger links with the leaders of those stakeholder groups that have an interest in the issue. It is vital that the community college become thoroughly knowledgeable about the stakeholder groups, including knowing their missions, goals, cultures, programs, and resources. The stakeholders, through their leaders, need to be encouraged to collaborate with the community college and leaders of the target public to define the issue, agree on the need to resolve that issue, and design and implement plans leading to its resolution as we noted with specific reference to adult illiteracy under Processual Task 7, above.

> ***Processual Task 9.*** *The community college initiates dialogue with leaders of the target public and stakeholders to encourage and assist these leaders in attaining consensus on the importance of the issue and in forming a coalition to address the issue.*

Identifying the leaders of the target public and the relevant stakeholder groups, while necessary, is not sufficient. Rather, the community college needs to develop within members of the target public and its leaders an awareness and understanding of the issue and how it affects the quality of their lives. The object is to attain *consensus* among individual leaders of the target public and stakeholders that the issue is important, is influencing the quality of life and well-being of the target public, and needs to be resolved. The outcome is a commitment from these leaders to collaborate in a coalition effort to confront and resolve the issue. Unless the issue is of major concern to the target public, and has been legitimized, the prospect of successful change is minimal. Statisticians, economists, and other experts may be well versed in statistical and quantitative trends, but they are rarely well informed about the culture of the target public and how it shapes their beliefs, attitudes, and behavior. Since processual tasks 7 and 8 in the community-based programming process have been undertaken by the community-based programming management team to connect the issue with its target public and stakeholder groups, it is essential that the final word on the importance of the issue come from members of the target public and stakeholder groups that it needs to be resolved. It is at this stage that a coalition of the leaders of the target public and stakeholder groups begins to come together.

> ***Processual Task 10.*** *The community college engages the coalition in further studying and analyzing the issue, refining the definition of the issue, and deciding upon the strategies to be pursued in resolving it.*

Generally, the defined issue is of a broad nature, touching upon many aspects of the life of the community—a macro issue—and so it will require further study, analysis, and refinement. Such study and analysis should concentrate on the economic, social-cultural, political, and technological factors that are influencing and shaping the issue. The goal is to learn as much as possible about the scope of the issue and to identify the subissues encompassed in it. The community college will need to assume a lead role in engaging and guiding the coalition in this critical examination. Once the coalition has reached consensus on a definition of the macro issue and its subissues, the community college will need to provide guidance for the coalition in defining the goal to be attained—that is, the creation of a vision that describes the ideal state of affairs that will characterize the target public if the issue is resolved. The goal becomes the focus toward which all of the coalition's future plans and actions for the resolution of the issue are directed. It is at this stage in its deliberations that the coalition turns its attention to the strategies to be pursued in resolving the issue. Each subissue will need to be carefully examined to determine appropriate strategies for its resolution.

Processual Task 11. The community college provides leadership for the coalition in translating its decisions into a unified plan of action.

The coalition, with the community college as its principal resource, is responsible for translating goals and strategies into a plan of action. It is at this stage in the community-based programming process that an educational action plan for resolving the issue is designed. This plan of action defines and describes the strategies that the coalition will need to use to resolve the issue. **It is the blueprint that guides the coalition's efforts and actions in resolving the issue.**

In designing the plan of action, the coalition will need to be helped by the community college to (1) state the macro issue in a succinct manner; (2) clearly articulate the goal to be sought in the resolution of the issue; (3) define and state each of the subissues; (4) formulate learner objectives to be achieved with respect to each subissue; (5) identify and describe learning activities that, when implemented, enable the target public to acquire the behavior specified in each learner objective; (6) develop a schedule for implementing the learning activities for each learner objective; (7) identify, define, and document the resources that will be required to implement each learning activity; (8) identify coalition members and others who will provide these resources and be responsible for implementing each learning activity; and (9) define and state the expected outcome to be attained for each learner objective.

This plan of action clearly details the strategies and actions of the coalition in resolving the issue. Of particular importance is the commitment that will have to be obtained from individual coalition members as well as other resource persons to play an active role in the unified plan of action by providing both resources and time to implement those aspects of the plan of action in which they have specialized expertise. These commitments should be documented in the plan.

> **Processual Task 12.** The community college aids the coalition in implementing the plan of action by providing consultation, technical assistance, and opportunities for coalition leaders and other community leaders to report on progress made, discuss obstacles encountered, and explore the use of alternative strategies not included in the initial plan of action.

The coalition has the responsibility for implementing the plan of action. The community college is responsible for guiding the efforts of the coalition in implementing the plans for resolving each subissue addressed in the plan.

The community college will need to provide the coalition consultation and technical assistance in helping it develop the operational strategies needed to function as a cohesive team. The coalition will also need the assistance of the community college in applying group process and other team-building skills to facilitate the interaction of its members. Of particular importance are the needs to help the coalition keep its efforts focused on resolution of the issue and to assist in obtaining the technical assistance from resource groups, other than those identified in the plan, that may be needed in implementing the plan.

It is important for the community college to help the coalition develop and implement a plan for monitoring and evaluating all of its actions.

Through planned formative evaluations, systematic monitoring, and interim summative evaluation, the coalition can gain valuable feedback and insights that will greatly facilitate its efforts in implementing the plan of action and resolving the issue. Only through feedback obtained from monitoring ongoing implementation activities can the coalition make informed modifications and adjustments in the plan of action, assuring its success in resolving the issue. Evidence of progress (or lack of progress) obtained through interim summative evaluation should be shared with the target population and stakeholders.

Finally, the community college needs to help the coalition develop and implement a plan for keeping the target public, stakeholders, and others fully informed about the coalition's efforts. It is important that these groups be kept fully apprised of results being obtained.

> **Processual Task 13.** *The community college provides leadership for the coalition in assessing the outcomes achieved toward resolving the issue and in determining the cost-effectiveness of the plan of action.*

The community college must make every effort to help the coalition determine the standards by which outcomes will be assessed and judged in resolving the issue. Once standards are determined, they provide an objective measure of the progress made toward resolving the issue. Results need to be documented, whether manifest, latent, intended, or unintended. The relation between input activities and subsequent outcomes needs to be examined for cause and effect. Goals need to be reviewed, compared, reassessed, and perhaps rewritten in light of the observed outcomes. The merits of the plan of action will depend upon how well it succeeds in resolving the issue in a cost-effective manner and also how effectively the experiences learned from it are used in future planning.

> **Processual Task 14.** *The community college arranges for and helps coalition leaders to report to their respective constituencies, agencies, organizations, and other stakeholders on the progress made toward resolving the issue.*

The issue addressed is integral to the overall quality of life for all people in the service area, and community-based programming is sustained by support of people who are not a part of the current coalition. Although other community leaders may not be directly involved in efforts at resolving the issue, they may well be involved in future efforts. Furthermore, as key people in the community, they are inextricably linked to the groups involved in the coalition, and their opinion is important. For this reason, they will need to be kept informed about the progress of the work of the coalition.

Those who participate as learners and providers in the program need and deserve to be informed about the results achieved. First and foremost, attention needs to be given to the target public and its leaders. Second, the stakeholders should be provided with information about the results of the plan. While these two publics will likely be represented on the coalition, their total membership needs to be informed of the results of the coalition's work. Third, the community college's leaders, faculty, environmental scanning committee, and governing board need to be informed about the progress made in resolving the issues. At the same time, although the primary task at this stage is to ensure regular and complete reports of the interim results of community-based programming, the interactive nature of the community-based programming process calls for an ongoing exchange of information for inspiration, for fact-finding, for problem-solving, and for decision-making by the community college, the target public, and stakeholder groups. In its role as catalyst, the community college assists the coalition in preparing regular reports to all those involved with the progress of and interest in the coalition's work.

> **Processual Task 15.** The coalition uses the results of the plan of action and lessons learned through its implementation to develop and implement new strategies for continued efforts toward resolving the issue.

The importance of the issue in relation to other community issues may change with the success of the action plan or with other changes in the community over time. Conversely, it may be recognized that continuing the work of the coalition is the most effective means by which the issue will eventually be resolved. In either case, a decision to continue or discontinue coalition efforts to resolve the issue will rest with the coalition.

The outcomes and lessons learned from this collaborative effort in working to resolve the issue inform and provide valuable information that can be used by the coalition as well as others in developing new strategies for resolving the issue or those aspects of it that remain unresolved. Insights as to which strategies worked, and which did not, can help to avoid obstacles in any subsequent efforts in resolving the issue.

The Critical Role of the Community College

Community-based programming is the pathway for the community college's entry into the twenty-first century. It can elevate the community college to a more central position in the affairs of its community than has ever been attained by any educational institution in America. **Through community-based programming, community colleges commit to working *with* the people rather than *for* the people. As neutral institutions, they commit to serve by working with the people, their leaders, and other community organizations to resolve critical issues in a time of unbridled concern over special interests. Community colleges commit to focus on applied knowledge as a key to unleashing the energy needed to rebuild America by solving problems in local communities.**

Today's pace of change is lightning fast. As John Gardner (1990) so perceptively put it in his treatise on leadership, we must "renew and reinterpret values"; we must "liberate energies and re-energize forgotten goals"; we must "achieve new understandings leading to new solutions"; and we must "foster the release of human possibilities through education and lifelong growth."

Community colleges are challenged to accept Gardner's premises and embrace the belief that empowerment can be a community-based process when it provides people from all walks of life with the opportunity and responsibility for developing their own innate leadership ability to its fullest.

What institution is better positioned to help people develop at the local level than the community college? What process is better suited to the task of transformational leadership than community-based programming? What community would not benefit from involving its citizens as participants in identifying and resolving significant issues?

Implementation of the community-based programming process will achieve significant social and economic changes that reflect the community of interests of both leaders and followers. The process is morally purposeful; it can empower the community college as well as the community; it collectively achieves a constructive dialogue between the needs and the wants of the followers and the capacity of leaders to promote shared understanding; and it builds a visionary social, political, and economic architecture upon the core values of the broad-based citizenry.

Skills Needed for Community-Based Programming

While the community-based programming process and its 15 processual tasks provide a systems approach for engaging the community college in resolving community issues, effective implementation of each of the processual tasks requires that community college leaders, faculty members, and community leaders become knowledgeable about and proficient in the use of community-based programming process skills. Among these skills are the following:

- integrating the concept of community-based programming into the total programming process of the community college;
- forming and using an environmental scanning committee;
- identifying and analyzing issues;
- studying, analyzing, and mapping target public(s) and stakeholder groups concerned with the issue;
- discerning and interpreting the indigenous knowledge base, culture, and social organization of issue-specific target publics, as well as the culture and social structure of stakeholder groups;
- accessing the target public and stakeholder groups by identifying and interacting with the leaders and spokespersons of the target public and stakeholder groups;
- involving the leaders of the target public and stakeholders in discussions about the issue within the context of their respective cultures, addressing how the issue is affecting the quality of life of the target public, and exploring with those leaders in the context of their cultures and social organizations, strategies for addressing the issue;

- forging the leaders and representatives of the target public and stakeholder groups into a functioning and viable coalition;
- facilitating the work of the coalition in reaching consensus on the issue and selecting collaborative strategies for resolving the issue;
- facilitating the work of the coalition in designing a collaborative and unified plan for resolving the issue, including formulating goals, devising strategies for achieving the goals, obtaining commitments from both the target public and stakeholders to provide the time and resources needed to implement the strategies, establishing a schedule for implementing the plan of action, and defining the outcomes to be attained;
- facilitating the implementation of the plan of action by the coalition, including continuous monitoring. Such monitoring should result in adjustments and changes in the plan as needed to assure success, namely the resolution or positive movement toward the resolution of the issue;
- helping the coalition assess the effectiveness of its efforts in achieving the expected outcomes; and
- supporting the coalition in developing additional plans if further effort is needed to resolve the issue.

To understand and become proficient in these skills, community college leaders, faculty members, and community leaders will have to master the content of and become skilled in system and culture analysis, group process, leadership development, coalition building, conflict management, consensus building, networking, and formative and summative evaluation.

Recognizing the inherent complexity of these 15 processual tasks, this book has been divided into 7 chapters, each devoted to a discussion of the concepts and the process skills needed by community colleges and their coalition partners to successfully address community issues. This book has been designed and is intended to serve as a resource in the vital work of building America's communities.

References

Gardner, J. W. (1990). *Leaders and followers*. New York: Free Press.

The Community College's Mission and Milieu: Institutionalizing Community-Based Programming

2

C hapter 1 introduced the community-based programming process as defined by the Academy for Community College Leadership Advancement, Innovation, and Modeling (ACCLAIM) at North Carolina State University. By placing the community college at the center of those organizations and agencies committed to improving the quality of life of their communities, the community-based programming process clearly defines the role of the community college as that of catalyst and leader for the next century.

This chapter discusses the community college's mission and the milieu that shapes and defines that mission. Understanding the community college mission is essential to understanding the significance community-based programming can play in assisting community colleges in fulfilling their mission. This chapter also places the community college's mission in historical perspective and emphasizes the necessity for each institution to define community-based programming in its own, unique context. As the chapter title suggests, community-based programming is an effective and efficient process a community college can use to achieve its mission without abandoning its historical roots.

Further, this chapter explores in detail the first three processual tasks in the community-based programming process. Understanding the first three processual tasks is necessary for comprehending the remainder of this work.

And finally, this chapter also introduces the concept of institutionalization. Because no process, including community-based programming, can reach its potential until it is incorporated into the college's planning process and ultimately into its culture, this chapter offers suggestions for institutionalizing community-based programming. The ultimate goal in the institutionalization process is to incorporate community-based programming into a college's culture.

A Brief History of the Community College

Many community college faculty, staff, and board members know little about the history of community colleges. The same is true of the community leaders who play a key role in the community-based programming process. While the following discussion does not provide a comprehensive history of the community college, it does present some important basic facts about that history. As is to be expected in a volume devoted to community-based programming, this brief history highlights the relationship of community colleges with their respective communities rather than other important relationships, such as those with students or universities. The information presented here also provides a starting point for more detailed readings on the history and mission of the community college's great and unique contributions to the nation's system of public higher education.

Today's public community college has strong roots in the nation's past. Borrowing heavily from the public high school, the private junior college, and the four-year college and university, the community college adopted characteristics of all of these, yet managed to develop its own identity. Influenced by such diverse forces as the Morrill Act of 1862, World War II, the baby boom following the war, industry's relentless demand for trained workers, and the civil rights movement of the 1960s, today's community college embodies Jefferson's beliefs that education should be practical as well as liberal and should serve the public good as well as individual needs (Vaughan, 1982).

Roots

The community college built upon the rich heritage of the land-grant institutions, including the "Wisconsin Idea," especially in regard to offering a diversified curriculum, serving the needs of the community, and opening the doors of higher education to ever-broadening segments of society. One result has been that community colleges today enroll more women than men, large numbers of ethnic and racial minorities, older adults, and practically anyone else who can benefit from attending the *"people's college,"* a term coined to describe land-grant institutions but today used to describe the community college.

The First Public Junior Colleges

In 1901, Joliet (Illinois) Junior College opened its doors to the public. (The term *community college* did not come into general use until after World War II.) Founded under the influence of William Rainey Harper, president of the University of Chicago, the Joliet College is believed by

Defining Characteristics of the Public Community College

While all community colleges have unique features, they also have certain common characteristics that define them. Some of these characteristics are described here.

Public Support: Community colleges are supported primarily by public taxes.

Open Access: Community colleges are economically and geographically accessible to people from all segments of society.

Committed to Teaching: Community colleges view teaching, not research, as their primary function.

Service Area: Community colleges serve a specific geographic area.

Community-Based: Community colleges consider meeting the needs of the people in their service area to be of primary importance.

Comprehensive Programs: Community colleges offer occupational and technical programs and courses, college transfer programs and courses, developmental courses, and credit and noncredit community service programs and courses.

Support Services: Community colleges offer personal and career counseling, financial aid and financial counseling, library and learning resources, and group and individual tutorial services.

many to be the oldest public junior college still in existence. The founding of Joliet Junior College was important because it demonstrated the feasibility and desirability of using public funds to establish community-based institutions of higher education, with the needs of the community helping to shape the courses and programs offered.

Public junior colleges found the rich soil and warm climate (political, social, and economic) of California to their liking. In 1907, California passed legislation authorizing high schools to offer courses constituting the first two years of a college program. In 1917, the state passed a law that allowed for local support for public junior colleges, and in 1921 the legislature authorized the establishment of independent junior college districts to be governed by local boards. California's 1921 act was a model for legislation in other states. Today, California has 107 public community colleges that enroll more than 1.3 million students in credit courses.

Early in this century, junior colleges, private as well as public, felt a need to join forces to articulate the role and mission of the two-year college in America. In 1920, a group of educators met in St. Louis and developed the concept of a national organization that would function as a forum for the nation's two-year colleges; in 1921, meeting in Chicago, these educators joined with others and organized the American Association of Junior Colleges to serve this purpose. In 1972, the organization changed its name to the American Association of Community and Junior Colleges to reflect more accurately the names used by most public two-year institutions. In

---

Timeline for the Development of a National Association for Community Colleges

1920   Idea of a national association of junior colleges discussed.

1921   American Association of Junior Colleges founded.

1972   Name of association changed to the American Association of Community and Junior Colleges.

1992   Name changed to American Association of Community Colleges. Current president: David Pierce, formerly chancellor of the Virginia Community College System.

1992, the name was changed again, this time to the American Association of Community Colleges, thereby symbolically depicting the community orientation of the public community colleges as they continued to dominate the two-year college scene.

The GI Bill

As World War II was winding down, the nation's policy makers struggled to determine what to do with the millions of armed services personnel who would soon return to civilian life. The answer in some minds was simple: send them to college. Consequently, the U.S. Congress passed the Servicemen's Readjustment Act in 1944. Known as the *GI Bill of Rights,* this act broke the financial barrier to college attendance for millions of Americans who had served in World War II. The public junior college and other institutions of higher education received tremendous boosts in enrollment as a result of the GI Bill. The GI Bill also set the precedent for today's student financial aid programs, firmly establishing the idea that students should not be barred from college attendance for financial reasons.

The Truman Commission Report

In 1947, less than two years after the end of World War II, President Truman released a report that would forever change the role, scope, image, and mission of the public junior college. The report of the President's Commission on Higher Education for American Democracy, commonly known as the *Truman Commission Report,* argued boldly that higher education plays a major role in preserving and enhancing the democratic ideals that the nation had affirmed through four years of global war. But the enemy this time was not the Axis powers. It was, instead, the barriers to higher education that the nation had erected over the years, especially in the case of minorities.

The Commission members believed that one important way to break down these barriers to higher education and in turn promote democracy for all was to establish a network of publicly supported two-year institutions. The colleges were to be called *community colleges,* a name that caught on at once and placed the community at the center of the mission of these institutions. Community colleges, the Commission claimed, should be within reach of most citizens, charge little or no tuition, serve as cultural centers for the community, offer continuing education for adults as well as technical and general education, be locally controlled, and be a part of the nation's higher education network while placing major emphasis on working with the public schools. The Commission made what at that time was a radical claim: 49 percent of the population could profit from two years of education beyond high school. The Commission's report placed the community college squarely in the center of the debate on higher education's role in promoting and interpreting American democracy (Vaughan, 1982), a position it continues to occupy today.

Many other laws, movements, and individuals influenced the development of the community college. For example, volumes could be written on financial aid legislation, beginning with the federal Higher Education Act of 1965 and its important amendments of 1972 and continuing with the ever-present Congressional debate on student financial aid. A long list could be developed of the important leaders of the community college movement. Included on the list would be national figures such as Jesse Bogue; Edmund J. Gleazer, Jr.; Dale Parnell; and David Pierce, all of whom have served as the head of what today is called the *American Association of Community Colleges.* Our purpose here is to concentrate on those aspects of the community college of most relevance to community-based programming, and it is with this focus that the history of the community college will be discussed.

From College to Community

As has already been illustrated, the idea that the community college should serve its community has a rich history. Early observers of the two-year college probably would be amazed at the breadth and depth of community college offerings today; nevertheless, they saw the public junior college as an institution committed to providing education for a broad segment of society in a wide range of disciplines and fields, including education for citizenship. For example, Leonard Koos, an early scholar of the development of the public junior college, noted in 1925 that these institutions gave students opportunities for experiences that constituted "laboratory work" for leadership (Koos, 1925, p. 23). Koos further observed that colleges located within commuting distance of their stu-

Comments about the Community College by the President's Commission on Higher Education, 1947

The President's Commission suggests the name "community college" to be applied to the institution designed to serve chiefly local community education needs. It may have various forms of organization and may have curricula of various lengths. Its dominant feature is its intimate relation to the life of the community it serves.

First, the community college must make frequent surveys of its community so that it can adapt its program to the educational needs of its full-time students. These needs are both general and vocational.

Second, since the program is expected to serve a cross section of the youth population, it is essential that consideration be given not only to apprentice training but also to cooperative procedures which provide for the older students alternate periods of attendance at college and remunerative work.

Third, the community college must prepare its students to live a rich and satisfying life, part of which involves earning a living. To this end, the total educational effort, general and vocational, of any student must be a well-integrated single program, not two programs.

Fourth, the community college must meet the needs also of those of its students who will go on to a more extended general education or to specialized and professional study at some other college or university.

Fifth, the community college must be the center for the administration of a comprehensive adult education program.

Source: President's Commission on Higher Education, 1947.

dents democratized higher education by making it available to members of the local community, thereby increasing the percentage of citizens who could go to college (Koos, 1925). Walter Crosby Eells, another early scholar, noted that colleges located in the communities from which they drew their students popularized higher education by making it available locally (Eells, 1931).

While these scholars did not advocate that public junior colleges be community-based institutions in today's terms, they nevertheless observed more than 50 years ago that local colleges should reflect local needs. Although the definition of what it means for a community college to serve its community has changed dramatically over the years, it is as true today as it was in the first half of the century that the effective community college continues to see its mission as primarily one of serving its local community.

While many other scholars and practitioners wrote about the community college in relation to its community, it is neither necessary nor practical to describe every such statement. It is, however, appropriate to look briefly at a book by Ervin Harlacher.

Catching the spirit of the times and the direction in which the community college was moving, Harlacher entitled his book, *The Community Dimensions of the Community College.* Published in 1969, it was one of the first books to describe the emerging community services movement that was becoming an increasingly important force shaping the community college mission. Harlacher noted that "the community college is a community-centered institution with the primary purpose of providing service to the people of its community. *Its offerings and programs are planned to meet the needs of the community and are developed with the active participation of citizens"* (p. 8, italics added).

Similar to the "Wisconsin Idea," in which the University of Wisconsin declared the entire state to be its campus, Harlacher suggested that "in a community college the campus is the length and breadth of the junior college district" and suggested that the community college recognize "its responsibility as a catalyst in community development and self-improvement" (p. 15). In regard to assisting the community, Harlacher stated, "The community college will increasingly utilize its catalytic capabilities to assist its community in the solution of basic educational, economic, political, and social problems" (p. 90). Harlacher captured the spirit of the times well; *community* was to be the key word in describing these community-based institutions.

Nineteen sixty-nine was a banner year for the community services movement in the community college. In addition to Harlacher's book, a monograph by Gunder A. Myran further defined the role community services could play in accomplishing the community college's mission. Myran (1969) made a strong argument for involving the community college in community activities, yet he kept the educational mission of the institution at the center of these activities.

The community college derives its primary legitimacy as an institution from its educational role; the community services division derives its legitimacy from this same role. The community college is not a governmental agency, a social welfare agency, a museum, a social club, a theater, a voluntary association, a religious institution, or a labor union. Community service in the community college is legitimate only to the extent that it is an extension or expansion of educational resources directed toward the social, economic, cultural, and civic needs of the community (p. 19).

Myran did not, however, limit the college's role to that of offering programs and courses, for he believed that the effective community college must assist in resolving the broad issues facing society.

Myran suggested that the college should focus some of its resources on working cooperatively with community organizations, agencies, and other institutions to improve the physical, economic, social, and political environments of the community (p. 15). Those resources devoted to serving the community, according to Myran, should not be the responsibility of one administrator or division but should be the responsibility of all areas of the college (p. 17). He reminded community college leaders that, even in the best of times, community colleges are unlikely to have the resources to "go it alone" when working to solve community problems (p. 32). He noted that organizations have the responsibility for meeting most of the functional requirements of society, including economics, religion, law, government, and education. These organizations exist in what he called "an interorganizational environment", and "this environment is the milieu" (p. 45) in which the community college functions. Linkages throughout this environment are critical, he noted. Sounding very current and rejecting the "all things to all people" syndrome many community colleges fell into in the 1970s, Myran noted that community colleges should not act unilaterally in attempting to resolve broad issues. "The community college will usually lack the resources necessary to tackle all but the most superficial of community needs, and…it lacks the social license to play an extended role" in solving these needs (p. 45).

In a well-reasoned analysis of the situation, Myran addressed the community college's role.

*It does not yet have the social license to use these resources for a uni-
lateral frontal attack on community problems which require responses
other than degree or certificate programs. Certainly the community
college can legitimately provide short courses, seminars, concerts,
etc.; these are important community services, but they cannot by themselves make an impact on the major problems faced by our nation.
That is why the college's greatest strength in this area lies in its ability to work cooperatively, through a community services structure within the college, with other community organizations and groups which
can also contribute human and physical resources (p. 45).*

Harlacher and Myran's observations and recommendations set the stage
for further thinking on the relation of the community college to its community.

The Community Services Movement

One individual who advocated broadening the mission of the communi-
ty college to place more emphasis on meeting community needs was Jesse
P. Bogue, executive secretary of the American Association of Junior
Colleges from 1946 to 1958. Drawing heavily on the Truman Commission
Report, Bogue carefully chose the title of his seminal book, *The Community
College.* He wanted to make it clear that the term "junior college" no longer
adequately described the emerging and unique institution committed to
serving its community, namely, the community college. Bogue asserted,
"The first qualification [of a community college] is *service* primarily to the
people of the community. The community institution goes to the people
who live and work where it is located, makes a careful study of the needs
of these people for education…, analyzes these needs, and builds its educational program in response to the analyses" (Bogue, 1950, p. 21).
Speaking directly to community needs, Bogue stated, "The community
itself has a real stake in developing and enriching its own life" (p. 69). In
Bogue's vision, the key to enriching community life was the community
college. He observed that "the community college performs the function
that helps to provide the more abundant life for the whole
community…[and] gives stability and richness to the national life of our
people" (p. 70).

Bogue's 1950 book was important, and it popularized the name "community college." It should be understood, however, that Bogue's vision of the community college's service to the community was primarily through providing courses and programs. His book gives little evidence that he saw the community college as a catalyst and leader in identifying and resolving broad-based community issues that could not be dealt with by the community college through formal courses and programs or through the community college acting alone. Nevertheless, he sought an expanded role for community colleges in meeting the needs of their communities.

James W. Thornton, Jr., author of a text widely used during the 1960s and 1970s in graduate courses on the community college, acknowledged the community college's role in preparing citizens to deal with community issues. He noted, "The community junior college is equipped to contribute significantly to the quality of citizen participation in understanding and in solving local and national problems. Avoiding partisanship, it can still encourage study, fact finding, debate, and the acceptance by citizens of responsibility for informed action" (1972, p. 254). As with other scholars before him, Thornton offered no process for involving citizens in resolving issues other than through an educational process consisting of courses and programs. Nevertheless, the idea of community involvement beyond the formal program is a thread that continues to weave through discussions of the community college mission.

From Community Services to Community Renewal

By the 1970s, community services had become an integral part of the community college mission, and the term *community-based* had become a part of the community college lexicon. The time was right for the community college to realize its long-held dream of being at the center of community activities, not just as purveyor of courses and programs but as leader and catalyst. Two books were published in which the authors advocated just that: the community college, to reach its potential, must be a community-based institution devoted to lifelong learning and community renewal and development, and it must be a leader and catalyst in this development.

The first of the books, published in 1976, was entitled *College Leadership for Community Renewal*. The authors advocated that the community college become a community renewal college and not just a college devoted to community services (Gollattscheck, Harlacher, Roberts, & Wygal, 1976). They suggested that each community college reexamine its mission and redirect it to assist in community renewal. Too often, they maintained, the expansion of services to the community meant the extension of conventional courses and programs to a larger number of students, contributing in part to the failure of community services to achieve its potential. The authors claimed that most of the emphasis on community-based education was little more than rhetoric (pp. 4–5). Their solution: the community college should become a community renewal college. And what would the community renewal college be? "Discarding the notion that certain dates, names, formulas, literary works, and atomic weights belong in everyone's intellectual kit,...the community renewal college provides a center for postsecondary education with emphasis on learner goals rather than institutional goals" (p. 11). "The community renewal college views itself as one agency among other social and civic agencies dedicated to human development and self-actualization.... The community renewal college must become an educational arm of the community" (p. 136). Little is new here: Harlacher and Myran's arguments covered this same territory and did so with arguments that are more refreshing and more persuasive.

The authors did not give up, however. They offered some sound advice about getting to know the community, although they knew of no model for a comprehensive community needs assessment (pp. 22–23). They brought some new thinking to bear on the role of the community college in chapter 3, entitled "Cooperating with Community Agencies." They observed that "communities are composed of diverse groups and individuals, and these components can seldom be drawn together in a concerted effort to prevent or reverse downward trends—unless a catalyzing agent consolidates and directs their energies. Such a catalyst is the community renewal college" (p. 44). The college, however, is only one of the many organizations that have as their goal community improvement (p. 45). The college, they suggest, does not have the resources to act alone (p. 46), but "as the agency with the broadest base of operations, the community renewal college should take upon itself the task of bringing the many community organizations and agencies into a working relationship" (p. 47).

Hence the college can serve as a catalyst in making organizations aware of the particular needs of other organizations' client constituencies and of each organization's potential for meeting these needs. Moreover, the community college can and should serve as a liaison in linking various community organizations in joint undertakings (p. 50).

While *College Leadership for Community Renewal* provided few new ideas for community college leaders to consider, another book did. Edmund J. Gleazer, Jr., served as the president of the community colleges' national organization from 1958 to 1981. During his long tenure, he did much to shape the thinking of community college leaders about the role of the community college. In 1980, shortly before leaving office, he published *The Community College: Values, Vision, and Vitality.* Here Gleazer set forth his vision for the community college. He began by questioning whether the word *college* should even be used to describe the public community college. But if the institution is not a college, what should it be? Gleazer's answer was that "the community college is uniquely qualified to become the *nexus* of a community learning system, relating organizations with educational functions into a complex sufficient to respond to the population's learning needs" (p. 10). Pointing out that community colleges have a tendency when addressing questions of mission to respond in terms of programs, Gleazer suggested "that the mission of community colleges be stated in this fashion: *To encourage and facilitate lifelong learning, with community as process and product*" (p. 16, author's italics). Gleazer warned that the community college cannot solve community problems alone; it must join hands with other community agencies and organizations. He discussed several examples of collaborative efforts being undertaken by community colleges and other community organizations.

Gleazer made important contributions to the thinking on the role of the community college in its community. He did not, as he pointed out in his book's preface, set out to write a "how-to-do-it" manual. He did, however, offer anyone interested in community-based programming much food for thought.

A Blueprint for a New Century

A 1988 report of the Commission on the Future of Community Colleges gives a more recent picture of the role of the community college in relation to its community. The report, entitled *Building Communities: A Vision for a New Century,* has been called a *blueprint for the next century* by David

Pierce, current president of the American Association of Community Colleges. The commission members placed the community college clearly at the center of community activities. The theme of the report is summarized as follows: *"We propose, therefore, that the theme 'Building Communities' become the new rallying point for the community college in America. We define the term 'community' not only as a region to be served, but also as a climate to be created"* (p. 7).

Clearly backing away from the traditional view of community services, the Commission called for the community college to form partnerships with other community organizations based upon shared values and common goals. Section Six of the report was devoted to "Connections Beyond the College." It used the litany of words and phrases that have come to be associated with the community college mission to describe the relationships: partnerships with schools, partnerships with senior colleges, and alliances with employers. This section, which comes the closest to placing the community college in the role of leader and catalyst, is summarized in the following quote.

> *The community college, at its best, can be a center for problem-solving in adult literacy or the education of the disabled. It can be a center for leadership training, too. It can also be the place where education and business leaders meet to talk about the problems of displaced workers. It can bring together agencies to strengthen services for minorities, working women, single parent heads of households, and unwed teenage parents. It can coordinate efforts to provide day care, transportation, and financial aid. The community college can take the lead in long-range planning for community development. And it can serve as the focal point for improving the quality of life in the inner city (p. 35).*

The Commission's report, which surprisingly failed to acknowledge the thinking of Gleazer, is helpful in understanding and appreciating the community college's mission, especially as that mission relates to building communities. This report, as is true with the other writings discussed in this section, did not, however, offer a process or a model for fulfilling the role of the community college as a community-based institution.

Number of Community, Technical, & Junior Colleges in the United States		Fall Headcount Enrollment at Public Community, Technical, & Junior Colleges	
Year	Colleges	Year	Students
1945–46	315	1945	216,325
1955–56	363	1955	683,129
1965–66	503	1965	1,152,086
1975–76	1,014	1975	3,921,542
1985–86	1,068	1985	4,597,838
1991–92*	975	1991	6,084,788

*Unlike previous years, only individually accredited colleges were counted, thus reducing the total number.

Source: American Association of Community Colleges, annual survey.

The failure of past works to offer practical ways of integrating college and community for the purpose of identifying and resolving issues gives added importance to community-based programming. Indeed, the ACCLAIM faculty, graduate fellows, pilot colleges, and hundreds of others committed to community-based programming are currently writing the next chapter in the community college's relationship to its community.

Understanding and Applying the First Three Processual Tasks

As discussed in chapter 1, community-based programming is a focused, results-oriented process that assists the community college in logically, effectively, and efficiently fulfilling its mission as a community-based institution. Since the process is a rational one, it is important to understand it from the beginning.

In the remainder of this chapter, we will therefore examine processual tasks 1, 2, and 3 in detail and within the context of the groundwork laid by earlier scholars, as previously discussed. It is important to keep in mind how processual tasks 1, 2, and 3 fit into the community-based programming model. *Most important, keep in mind that processual tasks 1, 2, and 3 have a symbiotic relationship and must be considered in light of that relationship. For example, it is not possible to develop a definition of community-based programming that is compatible with the institutional mission without first examining that mission.*

Defining Community-Based Programming

Definitions are important in understanding and implementing new concepts. It is especially critical that each community college define community-based programming in a way that is compatible with its mission. The first processual task addresses this key step.

Processual Task 1. *The community college develops and adopts a definition of community-based programming that encompasses those basic principles and concepts required to fulfill its mission as a community-based institution.*

Much of this chapter has been devoted to understanding the community college mission from an historical perspective, especially as the mission relates to interaction between the college and the community. Accepting the assumption that the community college is a community-based institution, let us now view the current mission from a perspective that brings the need for community-based programming into clear focus. Establishing the need for community-based programming is the first step in developing a definition that is compatible with a specific community college's mission.

Most community college catalogs contain a mission statement. In general, the mission states that the community college is an open-access, comprehensive institution. Most mission statements also include a list of functions or program areas (such as college transfer, technical education, developmental education, and community services) that reflect the focus of college effort. There may be some misunderstanding over the community services function, especially in noncredit offerings, and what it means to provide open access, but the mission is generally understood both by members of the college community and by the larger community. What is rarely understood, however, is how the mission, with its various components and concepts, connects with the larger community in an orderly, logical way. To understand this connection and the role community-based programming plays in making the connection, it might be helpful to look at the mission from a different perspective, keeping in mind that the purpose of processual task 1 is to develop a definition of community-based programming that is compatible with the college as a community-based institution.

To appreciate fully the mission of its community college, a community must see it as dynamic and constantly reshaped by a number of social, economic, technological, and political forces. What conditions have the greatest impact on the dynamic nature of the mission? How can community-based programming assist in deciding how the college interacts with those forces that help shape its mission? The following summary offers a new and exciting way of answering these questions in keeping with the community college mission.

Instead of considering the mission to be set with the focus on programs and courses, let us think of the mission as *dual-focused and dynamic* (Vaughan, 1991). Viewing the mission this way reveals why community-based programming can be an invaluable tool in assisting the college in achieving its mission.

What, then, is the dual focus of the mission? First, think of the mission as having an educational core. (*Do not* confuse the concept of the core as used here with courses included in the general education core.) The core is sound and relatively stable, with changes coming through the institutional planning process. It is the educational core that defines the community college as an institution of higher education; it is this core that is understood by the public and for which funds are appropriated by legislative bodies. Included in the educational core are degree, diploma, and certificate programs (one year or so in length, rather than weekend seminars or short courses) that constitute a coherent, integrated educational experience. Core programs may differ dramatically from one college to another, yet they all contain elements that distinguish the community college as an institution of higher education and set it apart from businesses, social agencies, and other organizations that provide training. The programs in the educational core have a starting point and a set of requirements, and they end with the awarding of a degree, diploma, or certificate. It should be remembered, however, that operating from the core, while extremely important, is only one focus of the community college mission. Nevertheless, stability in the core makes it possible for the other focus of the dual-focused mission to exist and flourish at most community colleges (Vaughan, 1991).

The second focus of the community college mission is at the edge of institutional activity. It is here that the community college most often interacts with society, scanning the environment and deciding what efforts to commit resources to and what to leave for others to address. The successful community college devotes resources to the edge as well as to the educational core, for the edge is where many of the innovative and exciting things are happening. The edge is where the community college intersects with its community and joins with other organizations, agencies, and institutions to identify and resolve broad-based issues that affect individuals and their communities (Vaughan, 1991). Many activities on the edge have the potential of being incorporated into the educational core. Moreover, many issues identified on the edge provide the community college the opportunity to serve as leader and catalyst in helping to resolve issues. (See Figure 1.)

To understand more fully the dual-focused mission, it is necessary to understand the process of assimilation. For the purpose of this discussion, *assimilation* refers to "the process of identifying educational solutions to ever-emerging, broad-based social issues, and incorporating these solutions into…course offerings," either credit or noncredit (Vaughan, 1991, p. 30).

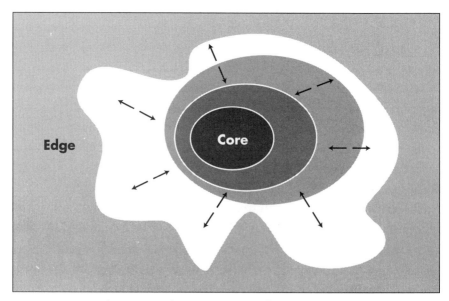

Figure 1. The community college's mission.

Recall that Myran cautioned community college leaders to keep in mind that the community college is an educational institution and not a social agency; therefore, its solutions to problems and issues must be educational. But by utilizing ACCLAIM's community-based programming model, the community college can and should serve as a catalyst and leader in resolving issues for which the solution is not always educational. For example, in those cases where the solution is economic, political, or social, the community college plays the role of catalyst, offering its educational services, staff support, and leadership, but leaves other organizations and agencies to play the major role in resolving the issue.

In addition to understanding the dual-focused mission and the process of assimilation, it is important to understand the relationship between the educational core and the edge. First, there is always tension between those activities in the core and those on the edge. The tension is a result of competition between the core and the edge for resources, including competition for funds, competition for attention, and competition to serve as the embodiment of the "real mission" of the community college.

This tension between the core and the edge causes the mission to stay in a constant state of flux. Existing in a state of flux is positive for the community college, for it forces it to interact with its community. One result of a mission in flux is its vibrancy; the mission is never permitted to "settle down" in the sense that the college refuses to take on new tasks.

Up to this point in the history of the community college, few institutional leaders have dealt with the activities on the edge of the mission consistently, efficiently, and in collaboration with other organizations. Often, leaders have ventured to the edge, in many cases through the narrowly focused vision and limited function of the community services division, and have *reacted* to what they found. They have found much more than any single institution can handle alone. The result has often been that community colleges provide job training or retraining for a specific industry rather than joining other organizations, institutions, and agencies in broad-based economic planning. Or community colleges view their role as limited to graduating nurses rather than collaborating with others to develop a comprehensive health-care plan.

These observations are not meant to criticize what community colleges have done in the past and are doing currently, for they have performed admirably on most fronts. Nevertheless, it is now time for community college leaders to evaluate their colleges' missions, to position their colleges to interact with broad-based issues in a structured way, and to join with other community leaders to identify, prioritize, and resolve issues that are having (or can have) an impact on the community's welfare. Once the mission is understood in this way, community-based programming not only makes sense, it becomes an imperative for the successful community college.

As stated in processual task 1, each institution should adopt a definition of community-based programming that is compatible with its mission. With the background presented thus far, that definition should be taking shape.

Understanding the Milieu

The following discussion emphasizes the need to understand the milieu in which the college functions, as there is a natural flow from definition to milieu.

> **Processual Task 2.** The community college engages in a careful study of its community to increase its knowledge of its social-cultural, economic, technological, and political environment.

No community college exists in a vacuum; as a community-based institution, the community college must interact with the sociocultural, economic, technological, and political environments in which it functions (Figure 2). To understand the role and scope of the community college, it is necessary to understand the milieu in which the college exists.

To open the discussion on the community college and its milieu, let us turn to the observations of Blocker, Plummer, and Richardson made more than three decades ago. "Institutions of higher education, which depend upon public support, cannot continue to be isolated from the mainstream of the social and economic system. These institutions, a part of the public domain, must respond to the needs of society in such a way as to preserve the best of the past and to contribute in every possible way to the

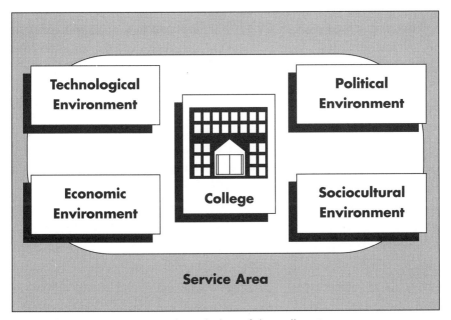

Figure 2. Increasing knowledge of the college's service area.

solutions of today's problems" (1965, p. 52). To respond to the needs of society and to engage successfully in community-based programming, community college leaders must achieve the goals of processual task 2: they must increase their knowledge about the social, cultural, economic, technological, and political environments in which they function. Another source notes that "the effectiveness of an organization is therefore contingent on how well its structure matches or can deal with the demands of the environment" (Bolman & Deal, 1991, p. 71).

The world has changed and continues to change at lightning speed. We face a technological revolution that gives us instant everything. A *Time* cover story is devoted to teenagers having sex; our world economy, with its emphasis on instant gratification, pushes us toward perpetual consumption; workers have part-time jobs with no benefits; record attendance at sporting events and movies are routine while church attendance is in decline; drugs on the streets and violence on television seem to permeate society; and these are just some of the changes in a society that is becoming increasingly diverse in its population and attitudes.

How can community college leaders understand what is happening and, once they make some sense out of it, utilize the resources of the college to help ensure that individual rights, responsibilities, and freedom are in concert with broader community needs? In the same vein, how do they ensure that communities respond equitably to the needs of all their residents and not merely to those with wealth or power? To answer these questions, it is necessary to understand the very basic segments of the environment that are constantly interacting with each other to produce a seemingly endless series of social, political, economic, technological, and cultural events that the successful community college must channel into avenues for community enhancement.

What is the sociocultural environment in which the community college exists? Obviously, it varies from college to college and from campus to campus. Yet the basic concepts of what constitutes the sociocultural environment hold from location to location. One source breaks down the social environment into demographics, life-styles, and social values (Fahey & Narayanan, 1986). Demographics are defined as the "size, age structure, geographic distribution, ethnic mix, and income distribution of the population" (p. 58). Life-styles are defined as those "patterns of living in the world as expressed in household formation, work, education, consumption, and leisure activities" (p. 73). While they do not define social values in the precise terms they use to define demographics and life-styles, the authors nevertheless point out that "values are the fundamental cornerstone of a society. Society's values are reflected in all its institutions, modes of behavior, mores, and norms" (p. 90). Some of the arenas in which values come into conflict are the political, regulatory, technological, social, and economic. Another source defines culture as "the pattern of beliefs, values, practices, and artifacts that define for its members who they are and how they do things. Culture is both product and process. As product, it embodies the accumulated wisdom of those who were members before we came. As process, it is continually renewed and re-created as new members are taught the old ways and eventually become teachers themselves" (Bolman & Deal, 1991, p. 250).

In relation to the community college, culture may be thought of as both process and product; it grows out of past and present action (process) and results in a set of shared values, beliefs, and assumptions about the institution (product). As suggested in the following quote, institutional culture goes down many avenues.

Culture consists of those things that make an institution distinct: its history, its traditions, its values, its interaction with the larger environment, its ceremonies, its renewal process (including the recruitment and selection of personnel), and its evaluation process (including the assessment of ethical values)...for example, admitting students who have academic deficiencies and not dealing with those deficiencies is ethically wrong. Such things as myths, legends, stories of the college's founding and of early institutional leaders are part of an institution's culture; they contribute to a sense of history and community and inspire loyalty to the institution (Vaughan, 1992, p. 2).

Understanding sociocultural, economic, technological, and political environments is a complex undertaking, especially as they relate to fulfilling the community college mission. But if we are to engage successfully in community-based programming, we must understand these environments, keeping in mind that once we enter the realm of values, "scanning is more difficult, complex, and precarious...than in any other environmental segment" (Fahey & Narayanan, 1986, p. 93). The operationalization of the concepts inherent in processual task 2 by the community college's leadership is mandatory for successful community-based programming. Without an understanding of the milieu in which the college exists, its leaders cannot successfully engage the institution in community-based programming.

With some understanding of the history of the community college and of the milieu in which it functions, we can move to processual task 3: deciding what, if anything, the college needs to do to position itself to engage in community-based programming.

Positioning the College

The next step in the community-based programming process moves the college from the intellectual world of definitions and environmental analysis to the active world of making changes in the college's mission, organizational structure, and goals (Figure 3). Relating the mission to processual tasks 1 and 2 is mandatory if the community-based programming process is to reach its potential as a tool for achieving that mission.

> **Processual Task 3.** *The community college examines and, if needed, reinterprets or modifies its mission, philosophy, goals, organizational structure, and mode of operation to emphasize community-based programming as one of its major programmatic efforts.*

Of the 15 processual tasks in the community-based programming process, none requires more forethought, planning, time, resources, and leadership skills than modifying or reinterpreting the mission, philosophy, and organizational structure of the college. Stated another way, these modifications should not be approached casually, especially modification of the mission. On most campuses, tampering with the mission is intruding onto sacred ground. Not only is the mission sacred, but modifying it is complex and time-consuming, and it involves changes in policy. Policy changes require approval of the governing board, and a policy change as near to the heart of the institution as its mission requires broad involvement of all segments of the college community, including community leaders.

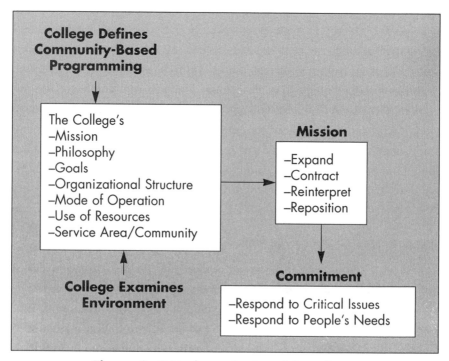

Figure 3. Critical examination of the college.

Why, then, would the community-based programming process even suggest that representatives of the college and the community consider carrying out processual task 3? After all, for most readers, the mission—at this stage of their thinking—might as well be on Mount Olympus, to be touched only by the gods (or at least the president and board). There are several reasons why processual task 3 is important to the community-based programming process and to the success of the institution in applying the model. First, the mission is a living statement that should be adjusted to its ever-changing environment. Second, few individuals ever look seriously at the institutional mission unless the institution is preparing for a regional accreditation visit. Preparing to implement the community-based programming process provides a reason and opportunity to review the mission, philosophy, and organizational structure in a less threatening environment than when the college is "under the gun" of an impending accreditation visit. Third, few opportunities arise to discuss the institutional mission and philosophy with community leaders. Introducing community-based programming provides such an opportunity. Finally, if community-based programming is to be an integral part of the college's planning process and ultimately a part of its culture, it must be understood in relation to the institutional mission, philosophy, and organizational structure. Bringing community-based programming into concert with the mission, philosophy, and organizational structure, with the ultimate goal of incorporating community-based programming into the institutional culture, cannot be accomplished unless those concepts and structures are clearly understood.

At this point, a college should apply what it has learned so far about its community and itself to the development of its mission statement. This task can be approached through a series of observations and questions.

The first step is to examine the mission and philosophy to determine if they incorporate avenues, either stated or implied, by which the institution can carry out its community-based mission. If the avenues are there and if they are understood and supported, then it is not necessary to modify the mission and philosophy of the institution; we can move directly to establishing goals for implementing community-based programming.

At this stage, establishing goals may seem to be little more than an academic exercise, for goals must become institutionalized if they are to assist the college in its community-based programming efforts. Institutionalization is discussed in the last section of this chapter; it is an important topic because it involves the institution's organizational structure and mode of operation. Nevertheless, if community-based programming is to be understood and carried out, it is important that goals be established.

If the mission statement and philosophy do not accommodate community-based programming, however, the task becomes much more complex. That complexity can be illustrated through a series of questions. For example, who is going to take the lead in modifying the philosophy and mission of the institution in ways that make them compatible with community-based programming? The obvious answer is the president. What can be done if the president is not a part of the group working on the mission? We must assume that the president has approved and discussed with the governing board the definition of community-based programming arrived at by the institution. We must constantly ask how processual task 3 relates to processual task 1 and how all processual tasks relate to the organizational structure and to other aspects of the college's operation.

It now should be obvious that processual task 3 cannot be carried out in isolation from processual task 1, for developing a definition of community-based programming that is compatible with the college's mission is mandatory and requires an examination of the philosophy, mission, and organizational structure of the college. For example, what does it mean to emphasize community-based programming as a major programmatic focus? In general, it means to apply the institution's definition of community-based programming to the college's mode of operation, making community-based programming one of the major components of the institution's planning process. Other questions come to mind. Is the organizational chart compatible with community-based programming? Who keeps the president informed regarding the daily activities inherent in the community-based programming process? If not, how are changes brought about? Who is likely to oppose these changes? On most campuses, faculty members are very sensitive to changes in the college's organization.

Is it clear who has the authority and responsibility for positioning the college in ways that are compatible with community-based programming? Most informed individuals readily admit that the president and board have the primary responsibility for positioning the mission. This being the case, what can the division chair, teaching faculty member, or community leader do to influence this positioning without appearing to dictate to the president and board or without appearing to meddle in the day-to-day operation of the college? Answering these questions is critical to placing community-based programming at the center of college activities. Successful community-based programming requires that the process permeate the entire college community; it is not just a function of the community services unit, of the president's office, of the environmental scanning committee, or of any other individual segment of the college. The relationship of community-based programming to the internal operation of the college is extremely important if the process is to become a part of the college's operation.

The mission should be examined in terms of its historical development and in relation to today's political, sociocultural, technological, and economic environments. Does the mission position the organization in ways that permit and encourage the college to collaborate with other community-based organizations? What restraints are placed on the mission by the governing board, the state legislature, or the institution's own bylaws? If the college is a member of a statewide system of community colleges, how does that fact affect procedures for modifying the institutional mission? The same question pertains to locally governed institutions.

What is the relation of the full-time teaching faculty to the community-based programming process? How can the regular teaching faculty become involved in the community-based programming process? Are the goals of the institution, including the goals of the teaching faculty, in line with the institution's definition of community-based programming? If not, should the goals be changed, or should the definition of community-based programming be changed? Is the philosophy of the institution one that makes it clear that the community college is a community-based institution? If so, do members of the college community understand what that means? If not, what steps can be taken to enlighten them?

The mission statement is the fountain from which all else flows. What does the mission statement itself say about the institution's being community-based? Many mission statements do not include a statement regarding the college's relationship to the community, leaving it to the community services arm to define the relationship—again, a mistake that confuses rather than clarifies the relationship of the college to its community. On the other hand, providing community services is an important function of the college, and its relationship to the community-based programming process must be clarified and defined.

These and other questions should be pursued as we seek to understand how community-based programming can be institutionalized and made an integral part of the institutional culture. As we embark upon a discussion of the institutionalization of community-based programming, keep in mind that only three of the 15 processual tasks have been dealt with in any detail up to this point and that suggestions for institutionalizing community-based programming will be an integral part of the subjects discussed in the other chapters. Also keep in mind that unless the first three processual tasks are understood, accepted, and implemented, it is unlikely that the remaining 12 will be carried out successfully.

Institutionalizing Community-Based Programming

We can have daily discussions about community-based programming, define it, relate it to the institutional mission, and understand the environment in which it functions. But until the process is institutionalized, little can be done to move the community college toward becoming a community-based institution. That is, institutionalization is the first and most important step forward in bringing community-based programming into the college's planning structure and is therefore the first step in incorporating it into the institutional culture.

Institutionalization, as used here, is defined as the process by which an institution incorporates changes into the structured and often highly formalized system that constitutes the community college as an organization. The goal of institutionalization is to incorporate changes into the organizational structure to such a degree that they become a part of the institutional culture.

With this definition in mind and recognizing that institutionalization is an evolutionary process, how can we bring about the institutionalization of community-based programming at a particular institution? The following are some of the key players and points to be considered in the process.

Strategies for Institutionalizing Community-Based Programming

In the foregoing discussion, it was observed that each segment of the college employs specific strategies to institutionalize community-based programming. A *strategy* may be defined as "the characteristics of the match that an organization achieves with its environment" (Fahey & Narayanan, 1986, p. 1). Any number of approaches may be used to achieve the match. If, however, they are to be effective and result in institutionalizing an undertaking, they cannot be in conflict with the institutional culture. For example, the community-based programming process would enjoy little success at St. John's College, an institution committed to residential life and the study of the liberal arts. On the other hand, the process is compatible with the community college and its commitment to serving its community.

In their discussion of strategy, Fahey and Narayanan refer to environmental analysis, not community-based programming, and to organizations in general, not specifically the community college. Their point, however, is relevant to the current discussion, for institutionalizing community-based programming in the community college requires that it be included in the college's strategy formulation process. In addition to the specific strategies suggested above, the following strategies will also assist in the institutionalization process. These strategies can be used in institutionalizing each of the first three processual tasks and indeed all 15 of the processual tasks in the community-based programming process.

■ Continually communicate to members of the college community and to the community at large the advantages of the college committing itself to the community-based programming process. For example, every time the college engages in a new undertaking, it should be demonstrated how community-based programming can assist in achieving the goals of the undertaking. This strategy builds a knowledge base for applying community-based programming to the college's activities and undertakings, both internally and externally. It also illustrates the necessity of learning the skills required in the community-based programming process.

■ Use every opportunity to teach the skills required to engage successfully in community-based programming. When the college develops a new program, community-based programming (processual task 3) requires that the external environment be analyzed and the knowledge be used in the program development process. For example, a new program in nursing should not be undertaken without a clear understanding of the health-care situation in the community.

■ Determine which individuals and groups can influence the institutionalization process, and involve them in all stages of that process. For example, who on the campus and in the community should define community-based programming (processual task 1)? What community leaders understand and influence the political environment (processual task 2)? What groups and individuals shape the college's mission (processual task 3)?

■ The most important single strategy a community college can employ in institutionalizing community-based programming is to integrate it with existing and emerging operations of the college. That is, community-based programming should not be viewed as an appendage of the college's operation; rather, it should be integrated into the college's governance and management when possible. An excellent example of how this objective might be achieved is related to analyzing the college's mission (processual task 3). The nation's regional accrediting bodies require that institutions seeking accreditation critically examine and analyze their missions. The accrediting associations do not tell the college specifically how this examination should take place or who should be involved in the examination. The college, in developing strategies for institutionalizing processual task 3, should integrate the examination and analysis of the mission as called for in the community-based programming process with the examination and analysis called for in the accrediting process. The community-based programming process opens the door for involving community leaders in examining the mission, something that should be done but rarely happens in the accreditation process. Integrating the community-based programming process with other activities at the college will result in institutionalizing the process and therefore making it a part of the institutional culture.

Strategies have little value unless they are carried out. Therefore, we will now consider ways in which various individuals and segments of the college community can enhance the institutionalization process. It is important to note again that institutionalizing any concept or change is extremely complex. Community-based programming is no exception. If it is to become a part of the college's culture, community-based programming must become a part of the daily operations of the entire college community.

Role of the President

Before any major undertaking such as community-based programming can be institutionalized, it must have the commitment and support of the president. Lacking that involvement, any discussion of community-based programming remains a futile exercise. The president is the individual on campus who has the primary responsibility for what is taking place and is the only one who has the ear and, one hopes, the support of the governing board. In addition, the president is the only one on campus who can marshall the resources required to bring about institutionalization of any concept. Once the commitment is made to community-based programming, the president can take several important steps to advance the institutionalization process.

- Understand community-based programming and communicate that understanding to the college community and to the community at large. This is the first and most important step toward institutionalizing community-based programming.
- Understand the institutional culture and propose that community-based programming become a part of that culture.
- Prepare the college community and the governing board for a commitment to community-based programming.
- Educate members of the college community and members of the board about the value of community-based programming.
- Engage vice presidents, deans, and other top-level administrators in efforts to promote community-based programming. Some aspect of the community-based programming process should be a subject at most staff meetings.
- Use informal as well as formal avenues in promoting community-based programming. As any experienced leader knows, the informal network can assure or block the adoption of a concept.

■ Use the weekly bulletin (or whatever communication medium is available) to keep the college community and the governing board informed as to the status of community-based programming on campus and in the community. This task includes providing new information and suggested readings as well as giving status reports on the process.

■ Use faculty meetings, board retreats, administrative council meetings, informal college networks, speeches to service clubs, and all other avenues available to discuss and ultimately promote community-based programming. Speeches given by the president on the general mission of the college should refer to its role as a community-based institution and to the role community-based programming plays in accomplishing that mission.

■ Assign a team to oversee the community-based programming process. The individual or team will be responsible for monitoring the process as well as evaluating its effectiveness.

Role of the Governing Board

The president and board are partners in any venture as bold and far-reaching as community-based programming. If community-based programming is to be successful, it must be endorsed and supported by the governing board, especially if community-based programming requires a change in policy, a major commitment of resources, a reinterpretation or repositioning of the mission, or a reshaping of the college's image in the community. The following are some of the ways the board can support the process.

■ Understand the value of community-based programming to the institution and understand enough about the process to discuss it with others and to raise questions with the president. Understanding must precede commitment.

■ Sanction the college's commitment to community-based programming. If the board is opposed to the process, it is doomed to failure.

■ Hold a retreat at which community-based programming is discussed in detail. Resource people (including the president, of course) who are well versed in community-based programming should be available to direct the discussion and to answer questions.

■ Support the president in efforts to institutionalize community-based programming. The support can be financial, moral, or both. Board support gives the president confidence to proceed at full speed and informs the college community and the larger community that the board is behind the college's efforts in community-based programming.

Role of the Faculty and Staff

Just as the support of the governing board is required, so too is the support of the faculty and staff. When community-based programming is discussed among select members of the college community, there is a tendency to forget that the faculty and staff ultimately must carry out many of the functions associated with the process. The entire college community, including faculty, secretaries, other support personnel, and administrators should work to institutionalize community-based programming. This commitment requires that all members of the college community be exposed to, understand, and be committed to community-based programming as both a set of beliefs and as a process.

■ Faculty and staff members must understand the community-based programming process if they are to support it. Once they understand the role of community-based programming in accomplishing the mission of the institution, they should be willing to "go public" with their support in ways that assure members of the college community that community-based programming is important to the college.

■ Faculty and staff members who participate in workshops and institutes on community-based programming must be willing and able to teach the process to members of the college community and community leaders who have not been participants. Those who have participated should serve as leaders and catalysts on campus in much the same way as the community college serves as leader and catalyst to its community in the community-based programming process.

■ Faculty and staff members must be willing to accept the changes brought about by the community-based programming process and must be willing to work with the president and board to institutionalize the process.

Role of the College

While it is awkward and perhaps even incorrect to talk about the college as an entity apart from the faculty, staff, president, and board, it nevertheless seems appropriate to view the college as a single entity and discuss what its board and personnel can do collectively to institutionalize community-based programming.

■ The college should define a series of goals that support the community-based programming segment of the mission statement. The goals should be published, and progress toward achieving them should be reported regularly.

■ The entire college community should participate in defining community-based programming and reach a consensus on the definition. This process can be carried out through established avenues (that is, the faculty senate and the administrative council) or through the establishment of a special task force devoted to developing the definition.

■ The college should incorporate community-based programming into its long- and short-range planning cycles. Inclusion in the planning process demonstrates a commitment to community-based programming in a way that is not available elsewhere; it also assures that community-based programming does not get lost in the institution's governance process.

■ The college should include community-based programming as an integral part of its governing structure. That is, community-based programming should be viewed as an important aid in governing the institution, especially in the decision-making process.

■ The college should involve community leaders, including local political and business leaders, in its community-based programming efforts. Workshops should be devoted to educating and involving community leaders in community-based programming. Community leaders should be included in the workshops conducted for members of the college community; otherwise, it is unlikely that community leaders can have an impact on the institutionalizing process.

■ Finally, the entire college community should work to integrate community-based programming into the institutional culture, taking every opportunity to include it in discussions of what the institution stands for and where it is headed in the future.

Staffing the Community-Based Programming Process

If community-based programming is to be institutionalized, the process cannot be left to fend for itself. For example, if the process is to become a part of the college's operation and ultimately its culture, someone must be responsible for seeing that it is successfully implemented. As suggested above, it is the college president's responsibility to see that the community-based programming process is not lost in the daily shuffle of running the college.

As discussed in chapter 1, if the community-based programming process is to be successful, the president should appoint a management team whose primary role is to facilitate the implementation of the process.

The team should consist of a small group of staff members who understand and are committed to the community-based programming process. The team should be chaired by a member of the president's administrative council, thereby assuring that the team has ready access to the president. It is also important that the activities of the management team be understood and supported by other members of the president's administrative council; therefore, the chair of the team should report on the activities of the team at each presidential staff meeting.

While the functions of the management team are discussed in chapter 1, they bear repeating at this stage, for without an effective management team the college cannot fully utilize and profit from the community-based programming process. Among the functions of the management team are the following activities.

1. Assist in institutionalizing the community-based programming process.
2. Assist the president and others in forming an environmental scanning committee and in engaging the committee in scanning the environment.
3. Oversee the work as the college analyzes and maps the target publics and stakeholders specific to a given issue.
4. Assist in identifying members of the target publics and stakeholders who have an interest in resolving a specific issue, and engage their leaders in a discussion of the issue.
5. Assist in forming a coalition whose purpose is to resolve the specific issue, and assist the coalition members in analyzing the issue.

6. Guide the coalition in its deliberations, and assist it in designing and implementing a plan of action designed to resolve a specific issue.
7. Assist the coalition in assessing the effectiveness of the community-based programming process.

In addition to the seven functions, the management team plans, oversees, and evaluates an ongoing program of staff development. At the center of the staff development process would be how to institutionalize community-based programming. To be effective, the staff development plan would involve all segments of the college community. While the management team consists of permanent members, it is important that the college utilize additional members of the college faculty and staff who can assist in the community-based programming process. By moving beyond the management team when desirable, the college gains additional resources and flexibility while maintaining consistency in its community-based programming efforts through its management team.

As suggested earlier, institutionalization of any process is difficult and gradual, and it may follow many different avenues, depending on the climate and culture of the college. Moreover, how effectively institutionalization is accomplished often depends on the importance of the concept, process, or program being discussed. Community-based programming is a process that will help the community college accomplish its mission as a community-based institution. Such a process deserves the attention of all members of the college community and should be institutionalized as efficiently, as effectively, and as rapidly as the college culture will permit.

Beyond Institutionalization: Environmental Scanning

This chapter discusses some of the ways a college institutionalizes the community-based programming process. The next chapter moves the process beyond institutionalization, indeed beyond the campus, into a detailed discussion of the environmental scanning process. Environmental scanning is important to the community-based programming process for a number of reasons.

Whether urban, rural, large, or small, today's community college is a complex institution operating in an increasingly complex environment. Effective community college leaders understand the need to anticipate changes in the external environment and to interact with those changes in ways that assist the college in achieving its goals. For these reasons, environmental scanning is an integral component of the community-based programming model.

The college's position as the originator and, to a large degree, the implementor of the environmental scanning process—and its position at the center of that process—clearly establishes the college as the leader and catalyst in bringing resources together to identify and rank issues. Moreover, environmental scanning moves the activities of the college's community-based programming process from the campus to the community, an important and mandatory step toward identifying and ranking issues. Identifying and ranking issues are the first major steps toward their resolution. We will now look at how environmental scanning fits into the community-based programming process and how a community college and its community can utilize environmental scanning to identify and rank those issues that threaten to engulf individuals and organizations if not dealt with effectively.

References

Blocker, C. E., Plummer, R. H., & Richardson, R. C., Jr. (1965). *The two-year college: A social synthesis.* Englewood Cliffs, NJ: Prentice-Hall.

Bogue, J. P. (1950). *The community college.* New York: McGraw-Hill.

Bolman, L. G., & Deal, T. E. (1991). *Reframing organizations: Artistry, choice, and leadership.* San Francisco: Jossey-Bass.

Commission on the Future of Community Colleges. (1988). *Building communities: A vision for a new century.* Washington, DC: American Association of Community and Junior Colleges.

Eells, W. C. (1931). *The junior college.* Boston: Houghton Mifflin.

Fahey, L., & Narayanan, V. K. (1986). *Macroenvironmental analysis for strategic management.* St. Paul, MN: West Publishing Company.

Gleazer, E. J., Jr. (1980). *The community college: Values, vision, & vitality.* Washington, DC: American Association of Community and Junior Colleges.

Gollattscheck, J. F., Harlacher, E. L., Roberts, E., & Wygal, B. R. (1976). *College leadership for community renewal.* San Francisco: Jossey-Bass.

Harlacher, E. L. (1969). *The community dimension of the community college.* Englewood Cliffs, NJ: Prentice-Hall.

Koos, L. V. (1925). *The junior-college movement.* New York: AMS Press.

Myran, G. A. (1969). *Community services in the community college.* Washington, DC: American Association of Community Colleges, Community Services Project. (ERIC Document Reproduction Service No. ED 037 202)

President's Commission on Higher Education. (1947). *Higher education for American democracy* (Vol. 3). Washington, DC: U.S. Government Printing Office.

Thornton, J. W., Jr. (1972). *The community junior college* (3d ed.). New York: Wiley.

Vaughan, G. B. (1982). *The community college in America: A short history.* Washington, DC: American Association of Community and Junior Colleges.

Vaughan, G. B. (1991). Institutions on the edge: America's community colleges. *Educational Record,* 72(2), pp. 30–33.

Vaughan, G. B. (1992). Scholarship and the culture of the community college. In J. C. Palmer & G. B. Vaughan (Eds.), *Fostering a climate for faculty scholarship at community colleges* (pp. 1–9). Washington, DC: American Association of Community and Junior Colleges.

Environmental Scanning

3

The previous chapter described the process of institutionalizing community-based programming in a community college. Essential to the success of this process is the full commitment of the governing board, the president, senior administrators, and faculty. Together, this process and a broad institutional commitment lay a strong foundation for the community-based programming effort.

Building on this foundation, the next challenge is to determine the issues that should be addressed through the community-based programming process. The choice of issues on which to focus is a critical element in winning the commitment of people in the community who need to be involved in the community-based programming process. Community-based programming is a collaboration between the college and citizens in its service area. Focusing on those issues that are of greatest consequence to the quality of life of the citizens will motivate community leaders to work with the college to resolve these issues. However, the success of the community-based programming process hinges not only on selecting the right issue, *but also on the way in which that choice is made.* The college must involve community leaders and others who are knowledgeable about the community, as they are the people best placed to make decisions about the issues. Thus, the next step in community-based programming is to collaborate with community leaders in a comprehensive and continuing investigation of the college's external environment, a process called *environmental scanning.*

Environmental scanning is the process of identifying, studying, and analyzing the current and emerging issues and forces that influence the quality of life of people in the communities of the college's service area. First, the process examines the issues that are highly visible in the media and in published reports that emerge through discussions with people in the community and that can be identified through personal observation. Data are studied to determine whether the issues are of sufficient concern to people in the communities to require attention and action. The issues are then ranked in priority according to the severity of their impact on these communities and the capacity of the community college and other institutions to address them successfully. On the basis of the information and analysis developed through the scanning process, those who conduct the scanning advise the president on the issues the college should address through community-based programming.

The following processual tasks carry the community-based programming process forward during this phase of the process.

Processual Task 4. *The community college's president establishes and employs an appropriate mechanism for scanning the college's external environment for the purposes of identifying and ranking, in order of importance, issues that are of critical concern to the community and its people.*

Processual Task 5. *The environmental scanning committee conducts a study of the community under the leadership of the community college president.*

Processual Task 6. *The community college's president seeks further confirmation and legitimation of the ranked issues from the college's governing board and from other community leaders.*

To carry out these tasks, the president establishes an *environmental scanning committee* as a standing committee of the college. Membership on the committee is drawn entirely from outside the college, with the president inviting 14 to 16 community leaders to serve on a committee that will become, in effect, the eyes and ears of the college. Through this committee, the college has the benefit of intelligent, inquiring people from the service area investigating significant issues facing their communities. The committee is an advisory body to the president and works closely with the college's community-based programming management team. The work of the environmental scanning committee is to conduct a systematic inquiry into the college's external environment across the whole spectrum of community life.

The environmental scanning committee provides essential information on which to plan for the future of the community and the college's role in that future. It consults with experts, monitors the media, studies documents and published reports, and interviews individuals and groups in the community. It is important, however, to understand that the environmental scanning committee's work is to gather information and to advise the president; it is not an action group. The community-based programming management team, which will work closely with the environmental scanning committee, is responsible for managing the community-based programming process.

Overview of Chapter

This chapter describes the components of environmental scanning within the context of community-based programming. It examines the processes of recruiting and training members for the environmental scanning committee, the methods by which the committee investigates current and emergent issues in the community, the committee's role in advising the president on the most significant issues, and the process by which the president negotiates the legitimacy of these issues with the governing board and local leaders as a focus for the college's work in community-based programming.

Definition of *Issue*

An *issue* is a matter of wide public concern that arises out of complex influences on the daily lives of human beings. Crime, unemployment, substance abuse, and a polluted environment are but a few of the issues that affect many American communities today. Issues have three key features: (1) they affect many people in the society; (2) they have their source in complex problems—economic, social, political, or technological—that are characterized by divergent viewpoints, shifting public perceptions, and turbulent values in an age of major change; and (3) they usually involve conflict, with resolution requiring mediation among competing interests. In community-based programming, the focus is on issues that adversely affect the quality of life.

The Environmental Scanning Committee

The environmental scanning committee serves the important function of carrying out the investigation into a college's external environment. The committee scans and monitors the social, cultural, economic, technological, and political environment to produce regular reports for the college and the community. The committee serves as a center for processing information about current and anticipated happenings in the life of the community.

At any time, many significant issues can affect the college's service area. The environmental scanning committee's task is to investigate those issues that are affecting the quality of life of individuals, families, and groups within the community. An important part of this work is to distinguish between the symptoms of an issue and the issue itself, a process that requires sustained investigation and analysis. The committee members collect information from such sources as television, radio, newspapers, official documents, and other publications, and also through discussion with experts and citizens in the community. They interview people through their own networks and, at times, commission special studies. The environmental scanning committee must be careful not to draw conclusions before it has made a thorough appraisal of the situation. When the committee has collected and analyzed enough information, it ranks the issues in terms of their consequence on the quality of life in the community.

Through the work of the environmental scanning committee, the community college

1. continually seeks information about the community college service area and the concerns of its people;
2. analyzes and records information in a systematic fashion;
3. identifies and ranks the issues that have a negative effect on the quality of life of people who reside or work in the service area; and
4. recommends those issues on which the college will work with the community to resolve.

Organizing the Environmental Scanning Committee

> *Processual Task 4. The community college's president establishes and employs an appropriate mechanism for scanning the college's external environment for the purposes of identifying and ranking, in order of importance, issues that are of critical concern to the community and its people.*

The environmental scanning committee is appointed by the president, and its work should be a function of the president's office. Although it is an advisory body, its members should be of such stature that the committee's recommendations carry weight and have credibility. Through these committee members, the college can gain access to significant sectors of the local community. For this reason, it is important that the committee represent the diversity of people within the community. It is also important to balance representation of stakeholders (including grass-roots leaders), not only to provide a broader perspective on events and issues but also to sensitize the college to potential conflicts between the various interest groups. Members can be drawn from a variety of sectors within the community: business and industry, education, health care, social work, government, and local citizen groups.

Selecting Committee Members

A college president begins the selection of environmental scanning committee members by consulting widely with the college staff, members of the governing board, and community leaders to identify potential members. The president will need to develop the terms of reference of the committee and be prepared to brief individuals on the role that committee members will play. The terms of reference should include the committee's purpose and objectives and should make it clear that the committee's overall task is to advise the president on the issues toward which the college should direct its community-based programming effort. Prospective members will want to know how frequently the committee will meet and the duration of their appointment. They will also be interested in knowing what support the committee will be provided in terms of resources and personnel.

The president should seek particular characteristics in committee members. They should be enthusiastic about the work and be prepared to give a significant amount of their time to the task. They should be capable of visionary leadership, knowledgeable about the service area, committed to continuing learning, and able to put the welfare of the total community above any particular sectional interest. Because the committee's work is a creative inquiry, members should have the capability to listen to and learn from others. The committee should also reflect the diversity of the area in terms of gender, ethnicity, geographic distribution, and status within the various communities.

From the list of nominees, the president selects and invites individuals to serve on the committee. Although the members of the college's community-based programming management team will work closely with the environmental scanning committee, they are not members of the scanning committee. Members of the management team will attend meetings of the environmental scanning committee, but their role is to facilitate the proceedings and provide assistance to the committee members, not to engage in gathering and analyzing information or making recommendations.

Training Committee Members

In the initial meetings of the committee, attention should be given to developing relationships among members to form a functioning group and to training the members for the task of environmental scanning. If practical, conducting a one-day workshop would get the committee off to a good start. This session would not only make it possible to brief the members on their task but would also provide an opportunity for them to work together and establish a good working culture for the group. The committee has a demanding and complex task, and yet the majority of members will be volunteers. The issues to be discussed will frequently be contentious. To manage the committee's processes effectively, the chairperson—often the president or the vice-president of the college—will want to work toward developing a purposeful and task-oriented group. Ideally, members should look forward to the meetings. In planning the initial training session, the chairperson should consider not only briefings on community-based programming and environmental scanning but should also address the skills needed for working effectively in a group and the techniques of inquiry that members will use in their investigations. Of particular importance is training members to work with consensus as their decision-making technique.

Not all of this training must be accomplished at the beginning. Special training sessions on particular topics can be organized later in the process. The essential topics to be covered in training are

- community-based programming;
- environmental scanning;
- the function and tasks of the scanning committee;
- operating procedures for the committee;
- community life categories (to be discussed later in this chapter);
- sources of information;
- methods of collecting data (interviewing, published documents, the media, and research); and
- identification, analysis, and ranking of issues.

In character with the collaborative philosophy of community-based programming, the training sessions should be participative in nature. Some topics, such as *community-based programming,* are best handled by straightforward presentations. Others, however, such as operating procedures for the committee, methods of collecting data, and sources of information, are better approached in a participative way. It is a good idea to develop a list of information sources through a brainstorming session. A basic list will include

- community leaders,
- public records,
- newspapers,
- census reports,
- economic surveys, and
- unemployment reports.

The chairperson has an important task in developing a purposeful yet convivial working ethos in the group. In the early meetings, when the basic culture of the group is forming, he or she should strive to establish conditions in which all members feel valued and free to participate. Members need to know that the others are listening to them and that their views are respected. The college members can provide a valuable group maintenance function in such situations through the use of their skills in the team-building process.

Role of the College and Its Community-Based Programming Management Team

The members of the community-based programming management team perform a valuable function when they attend meetings of the environmental scanning committee; they can apply their skills in group process. They have a particular responsibility for supporting the contributions of committee members. Later in the process, when the scanning committee is organized into community-life category study groups, members of the management team should be assigned to each group to provide administrative support and technical assistance.

Environmental scanning is a major task. Many organizations employ full-time professionals to do this work, yet in community-based programming the community college deliberately draws upon volunteers from the community. It is important that the committee members do not feel overwhelmed by the task. They can be much encouraged by the professional support the college can provide. Secretarial, clerical, and computing assistance is an important part of that support.

Studying the Community

Processual Task 5. The environmental scanning committee conducts a study of the community under the leadership of the community college president.

Environmental scanning focuses on developing a greater sensitivity to the changing external world of the college. It is concerned with identifying current and future issues that will affect the community and the college. Members of the environmental scanning committee must therefore be in tune with and able to articulate the concerns of the people in the community. To do so, the committee must investigate a wide variety of sources and pool the experience of its members. The committee addresses the following questions.

1. What is happening in the college's service area, and what are the likely developments in the future? What are the issues, and how do they affect the lives of people in the local communities?
2. Who is involved in and affected by the issues?
3. What is the scope and severity of each issue?
4. What are the environmental factors, such as the social, political, economic and technological forces, that are shaping the main issues?

Using Community-Life Categories to Organize the Investigation

The intent of the scanning process is to develop as comprehensive an appraisal of the college's current and future environment as possible, given the resources available. Clearly, the committee can draw upon many sources of information on all aspects of the community's life. The problem is deciding where to direct the effort, so committee members do not become overwhelmed by a vast amount of seemingly unconnected data. Fortunately, the committee can benefit from the experience of social statisticians, who have already considered the problem, and organize the investigation according to *community-life categories.*

Fitzsimmons and Lavey (1976) developed a comprehensive community-level assessment procedure that provides a useful framework for the environmental scanning process. It was designed to enable people to understand how public investment affects the quality of life of individuals and the social well-being of the community. Their community-life categories make it possible to assemble data so as to give structure to the functioning of the whole community. Their purpose in developing the community-life categories *"was to permit description at specific points in time of the characteristics of community residents, the institutions which serve them, and the activities which affect their lives"* (Fitzsimmons & Lavey, 1976, p. 392).

Fitzsimmons and Lavey recommend 15 community-life categories:

1. Education.
2. Economic base.
3. Employment and income.
4. Welfare.

5. Government operations and services.

6. Transportation.

7. Law and justice.

8. Environment.

9. Social services.

10. Recreation and leisure.

11. Housing and neighborhood.

12. Transportation

13. Communications.

14. Religious life.

15. Family life.

These community-life categories are defined in Table 1.

Table 1. Community-Life Categories and Their Definitions

Education: All persons seeking the development of formal knowledge and skills together with the institutions and organizations, either public or private, which serve these needs.

Economic Base: All activities of industry, agriculture, commercial operations, and other businesses which produce or provide goods and services.

Employment and Income: All persons seeking jobs in whatever occupation within the economic base, the jobs available to them, and the income earned by them.

Welfare: Needy persons, such as the elderly, families with dependent children, and the disabled, and the institutions engaged in the provision of income and/or services to them.

Government Operations and Services: The structure of local government and its operations in response to community needs, including providing public services, creating ordinances, and organizing activities.

Law and Justice: Persons violating the law, the damage done by them, and the operation of the police, courts, jails, and lawyers to protect the residents, enforce the laws, provide fair and speedy trials, and establish efficient, remedial detention of those convicted.

Environment: The availability and protection of natural resources, wildlife, and land and water for use by all living things, the persons and groups concerned with these causes, and the activities and provisions regarding these causes.

Health: The physical and mental well-being of residents and the activities and services of all health-related personnel and facilities designed to maintain and promote good health and to provide treatment for those in need.

Social Services: Persons seeking services to lead a more rewarding and enjoyable life and the provision of those services, such as adoption, boy scouts, and vocational counseling.

Recreation and Leisure: The presence and opportunity to participate in the leisure-time recreational and cultural activities of one's choice and to achieve the benefits derived from participation, and the person engaged in those activities.

Housing and Neighborhood: Persons residing in the community, the availability and characteristics of housing units, and the quality of neighborhoods.

Transportation: Persons and goods moved by car, bus, train, plane, boat, or other means within the community and between communities, and the quality and costs of transportation.

Communications: Persons engaged in sending and receiving information and the availability and quality of various forms of communications-oriented services.

Religious Life: The presence of and opportunity to attend the religious services of one's choice and to achieve the benefits derived from those practices, and the persons engaged in those activities.

Family Life: Persons living in and benefitting from families and the relationship of the individual to the community as a family member.

Source: Adapted from Fitzsimmons and Lavey (1976).

The scanning committee may not feel it necessary to investigate all of these community-life categories and may want to concentrate its efforts in areas where it is already aware there are pressing issues. In that case, this schema could be simplified by aggregating several of Fitzsimmons and

Lavey's categories. (For example, "economic base" could become "economic base, employment, and income.")

Although the selection of community-life categories and the organization of data by these categories can be approached systematically, the community should remember that environmental scanning, by its very nature, is an inexact and sometimes ambiguous activity. The range of what might be regarded as relevant data is unlimited. Many potential items of data are invariably scattered and imprecise, and sources of data are many and of varying quality (Fahey & Narayanan, 1986). The environmental scanning committee should give thought to these issues but need not be unduly concerned with making a perfect choice of community-life categories around which to organize its investigation.

A challenge for the committee is to make sense of the data, much of which will be imprecise and appear unconnected. This task will engage not only the members' capacity for logical analysis but also their intuition and creativity. The outcome of the process is to identify and provide a preliminary analysis of the most significant issues that the college can choose to address through community-based programming. It is not catastrophic if the committee misses or misunderstands an important issue after the first round of its investigation because there are inherent checks in the community-based programming process. If the issue is highly important, there will come a time when the scanning committee will register the issue's significance as the process of scanning and monitoring the college's external environment continues.

Using Study Groups to Conduct the Investigation

The environmental scanning committee can be organized into *study groups* assigned to investigate various community-life categories. An advantage of this approach is that it enables the committee to explore in depth many aspects of community life. It enables the meetings of the scanning committee to focus on the broad picture and not become bogged down in the details of data collection and analysis. In addition, being a part of a smaller group provides support and motivation for the volunteer members.

The study groups can use a wide range of methods for their investigations. The main techniques will be interviewing people in the college's service area and gathering data from published sources. It may be appropriate later to organize a specific research study. For example, members of a study group investigating the community-life category "education" may quickly learn that although ample information is available about formal education programs, little information can be obtained about nonformal education. In the absence of information about what local companies and state organizations provide in the way of training, the study group therefore may decide to conduct a survey to gain more information.

Interviewing local people is an important source of information about the issues that are currently troubling the community. Clearly, the issues that people say are important should be given close attention. A word of warning, however, should be offered as to the subjective character of the data collected through interviews: sometimes the information provided and views expressed are based on misunderstandings and erroneous reports. Although interview data are important, they must be treated with caution and certainly must be supplemented with data from other sources, so an accurate picture of the issue can be drawn. Study group members should gather reports and keep a record of their contacts. Later in the community-based programming process this information and the committee's contacts will be invaluable to the community-based management team and coalition formed to address a specific issue.

Some community-life categories may already be under investigation by other organizations and agencies. There are likely to be experts in the area whose work it is to develop good information about specific community-life categories. The members of the scanning committee should therefore establish contact with these experts, and it may be useful to invite these experts to talk to the full committee.

Examples of Issues Affecting Communities

An issue affecting a number of American communities in a period of defense spending cuts is the loss of jobs in the defense industry. For example, many jobs have been cut in naval shipyards, producing a drastic effect on nearby communities. Losing their jobs affects the workers, their families, the local shops, and the small businesses that served the shipyards. This is an example of a significant issue that the environmental scanning process would reveal to be a priority.

However, if we consider as an example the matter of health care in two very different communities, we can understand that an issue of great importance in one community may be of much lesser consequence in another. Suppose that in the first community the majority of people are wealthy and have good health-care insurance. There are enough doctors, hospitals, and other health-care facilities. Although there are a small number of people who cannot afford adequate health care, as far as the community college is concerned they do not constitute a large enough public to warrant a community-based programming initiative. In the second community, the story is very different. A large number of people there cannot afford to pay for health care, and the health-care services available locally are inadequate. The quality of people's lives is affected by poor health. Other groups also have a stake in this issue, such as health departments and local employers who are concerned about their employees' poor health. In this community, the conditions are right for the local community college to focus its community-based programming efforts on the health-care issue. Examples of issues that exist in nearly every community in the nation are;

- ■ economic development (for example, unemployment, workforce preparedness, and development of small businesses);
- ■ health care (for example, access, preventive practices, and substance abuse);
- ■ adult literacy;
- ■ crime;
- ■ the environment (for example, waste disposal, pollution, and the cost of vandalism); and education (for example, school dropouts, student performance, and violence in the classroom).

Identifying, Evaluating, and Ranking the Issues

Even the simplest environmental scanning system will quickly identify more emerging issues than can be handled by the college's community-based programming effort. At some point it becomes necessary to reduce the total to a manageable number. This limiting process should be as rational and unbiased as possible. The chairperson's task is to create a procedure through which the committee can, by consensus, rank the issues and single out those for immediate attention by the college.

The task of the environmental scanning committee is not to develop ways of resolving the issue. It is not to engage in problem solving because that process comes later when representatives of the target public and stakeholders have been brought into the process. For practical purposes, however, the committee does need to assess how feasible it might be for the issue to be resolved through community-based programming. An especially intractable issue would not be given a high priority when there are other issues that could be resolved more readily through community-based programming.

Deciding which issues to advise the president to consider as a focus for community-based programming is a critical judgment. There are several ways in which a group can make decisions. The most important of these for the scanning committee is *consensus decision making through open discussion.* At first, the process of consensus decision making takes considerable time and is hard work. As the group continues to work together, however, the members gain confidence in the method and become more adept at the process.

The process of reaching consensus can be better understood if we consider the alternative ways in which a group can reach a decision: by authority, minority, majority, consensus, and unanimous agreement (Schein, 1988). Each of these modes of decision-making is appropriate under particular circumstances. They have their particular advantages but also certain drawbacks.

Decisions can be made by authority when the leader of the group has the formal authority to make decisions or, in the case of a committee, the chairperson is given the authority to act on its behalf by the members. Decision-making by one person has the great advantage of speed, but the drawback is that the quality of the decision depends on the competence of the individual. In complex decision-making situations, relying on one person's judgment is risky. Furthermore, when all the important decisions are made by one person, the other members of the group can develop a dependent mentality, and the group's capacity for effective analysis of the situation is considerably impaired.

Decisions can be made by a minority of group members, as may happen when those members have some special expertise that the group relies upon or when a subgroup has maneuvered itself into a position to influence the group as a whole. Minority decision-making also has the advantage of speed. However, when it becomes a dominant mode for the group, it may engender unsatisfactory psychological dynamics that will impair the quality of the group's work. The other members can feel manipulated and become angry, and trust in the group can deteriorate. These dynamics may also be expressed through members' apathy and their diminished contribution.

Majority decision-making is also a quick way to make a decision after discussion. On occasions when no consensus has been reached, it may be appropriate to call for a vote. However, resorting frequently to voting can foster an unhealthy group dynamic. Generally, the same members will repeatedly be in the minority camp, which can lead to antagonism, frustration, and alienation. Meetings may well become acrimonious, and members may act out their feelings by coming late or not attending. (See chapter 4 for a discussion of group development.)

For the particular nature of the scanning committee's work, reaching consensus is the most appropriate way of making decisions. Seeking consensus requires that favorable conditions exist in the group for the necessary discussion. The group must conduct a debate in which all members have the opportunity to argue their point of view and feel that they will be heard by the others. The members should understand that in complex decision-making situations no one person will have all the information needed to arrive at the best conclusion. The most effective method is for people to share what they know and use their intelligence collectively. Consensus decision-making depends heavily on effective communications within the group. Members must have the opportunity to speak, and the others must listen. Members must respect their colleagues and be prepared to be influenced by new information or a sound argument. The group's capacity for analysis and criticism must be balanced by support and encouragement for each other's contributions.

Keep in mind that it is not necessary in consensus decision-making that every individual be completely convinced by the argument, but only that after adequate discussion all members can be committed to the group decision because they trust the procedure. Under these circumstances, a scanning committee can use group discussion to arrive at sound decisions.

As the environmental scanning committee carries out its work, each study group will identify a number of important issues within its community-life category. The study groups will make a preliminary assessment of the importance of these issues to the quality of life of people in the community. They will then report to the main committee, providing a rank-ordered list of issues. The environmental scanning committee will consider all the reports from the study groups and then make a collective ranking of the issues. It is important that the members take a broad view and not identify only with their particular study group when arriving at this final judgment. The environmental scanning committee is then in a position to advise the president on the issues that, if addressed through community-based programming, will have the greatest effect in improving the quality of life of people within the college's service area.

Confirming and Legitimating Issues

Processual Task 6. The community college's president seeks further confirmation and legitimation of the ranked issues from the college's governing board and from other community leaders.

The next task is for the president to consult formally and informally with leaders in the community. Before proceeding further with community-based programming, the president needs to secure the support of community leaders, particularly the governing board of the college. The environmental scanning committee's advice is based on a wide sampling of public opinion and the factual information gathered in the investigation. However, to avoid any misunderstanding and unnecessary opposition, it is important that the president discuss the college's role in addressing the top-ranked issue with the established leadership in the community. These leaders wield considerable influence that they can use to either block or support the college's work. They can verify the recommendations of the environmental scanning committee, and they can legitimate the college's work on the issues. Their backing will be an important source of strength to the community-based programming process.

The governing board, of course, constitutes a special group of leaders for the college. It bears ultimate legal responsibility for the affairs of the college. The board establishes the college's framework of policy, and the members of the board certainly need to consider the implications of any major initiative that the college plans to undertake in the community. It is clearly very important that the groundwork be laid for this dialogue by involving the board at an early stage in community-based programming and by winning its backing for the concept. The president's task in seeking support to address a specific issue is much more difficult if the board has not already gained a good knowledge of community-based programming and has not agreed to adopt it as a tool for working within the community. If the board is already familiar with and committed to community-based programming, the president can concentrate on making a case that the specific issue is of major significance to the community and that the college has an important contribution to make toward resolving the issue.

It is important to approach discussions with community leaders as a two-way process. The president can learn much from leaders' perspectives on the issue. If the environmental scanning committee has done a good job in identifying and characterizing the issue, the leaders will usually welcome the initiative and give the president their support.

Continuing the Environmental Scanning Process

Delivery of the scanning committee's first report is in a sense a watershed event, marking a transition in the life and work of the committee. During the period when the report is being developed, many members will be very busy and will show considerable enthusiasm for and satisfaction in the group's achievement. Inevitably, there will be a feeling of anticlimax after that initial effort has been completed. The scanning committee must continue its work, however; indeed, it has an important continuing function in the life of the college. Yet, the pace of the work will slow in the period during which the college assimilates the first report and until the college has the spare capacity to consider further community-based programming initiatives. The chairperson must be prepared for this transition and work to maintain the committee members' continuing involvement and commitment. He or she will need to establish new goals for the committee. The schedule of meetings should be adjusted because the group will need to meet less frequently. Also, members must be kept informed about developments in the community-based programming process. Regular updates on the college's community-based programming activities will be an important source of inspiration for the committee members' continuing effort.

When an issue has been identified and agreed upon as one toward which the college will direct its community-based programming effort, the president must take the next step. It is not the function of the environmental scanning committee to manage the community-based programming initiative. The responsibility for further work on the issue now rests with the president, and at this point he or she delegates responsibility to the community-based programming management team.

The Next Phase: Study, Analysis, and Mapping of the Target Publics and Stakeholders

On the basis of the environmental scanning committee's report, the president and the community-based programming management team establish an issue that the college will address through community-based programming. The president then secures the backing of local leaders and the governing board. By this time the college has learned a great deal about the community, but there is much more to learn before the college can begin to organize a coalition of members from the target public and stakeholders who will begin to seek ways to resolve the issue that the community college has selected for its initial efforts. Members of the community-based programming management team therefore *begin to study, analyze, and map* the target public and stakeholders affected by the issue (processual tasks 7, 8, and 9). Their first objective is to gain an appreciation of the special culture of the target public, so they can come to see the issue through the eyes of the people most directly affected. In this way they can establish a basis for an authentic dialogue in which the voices of the people have authority. Their other, more specific objectives are to locate the leaders in the community who can effectively speak for the target publics and the leaders who can represent the stakeholders. These processes are described in detail in chapter 4.

References

Fahey, L., & Narayanan, V. K. (1986). *Macro environmental analysis for strategic management.* St. Paul, MN: West.

Fitzsimmons, S. J., & Lavey, W. G. (1976). Social economic accounts system (SEAS): Toward a comprehensive community-level assessment procedure. *Social Indicators Research,* 2, pp. 389–452.

Schein, E. (1988). *Process consultation.* Reading, MA: Addison Wesley.

Identifying Target Publics and Stakeholders: Building a Coalition

4

The two preceding chapters discussed the tasks of (1) institutionalizing community-based programming as an integral component of the community college's mission and operations and (2) forming an environmental scanning committee and engaging it in identifying and ranking issues of critical concern to the community and its people. After the environmental scanning committee has identified and ranked the issues according to the severity of their impact, the college president obtains from the college's governing board and other community leaders confirmation of the issues and legitimation of the college's involvement in addressing the issues through community-based programming.

At this critical juncture, the college selects one issue on which to focus its community-based programming efforts. A single issue is selected so as to provide college staff and community members the opportunity to concentrate their energies and to learn and grow together in their understanding of community-based programming. During the initial phase of community-based programming, a great deal must be learned by all participants, both on and off the campus. This learning is best accomplished by focusing energies on an achievable goal. Once this issue has been addressed successfully, more than one issue may be taken on by the college at any time. All the processes described in this chapter must still be applied to *each* issue, as there are distinct target publics and stakeholders for each issue.

Once an issue has been selected, all subsequent processual tasks focus on initiating and effecting collaboration with those who are affected by the issue. The aggregate of people who are directly and adversely affected by the issue constitute a special population called the *target public,* and change in their knowledge base and practices is critical to the successful resolution of the issue. For each issue, there is one distinct target public. This population is most significant to community-based programming, but historically it has been neglected in the planning process. Since the resolution of the issue rests in a change in the target public, its members *must* be directly involved in determining what must change and how the change will be brought about. In addition to the target public, other individuals, groups, organizations, and agencies who have a stake in the issue and an interest in the target public—referred to as *stakeholders*—must also be involved in the resolution of the issue. Many of the stakeholders may already be providing programs in an attempt to address the issue, and their expertise and resources are needed to resolve the issue. They must, however, develop a commitment to collaborate with each other and with the target public in developing and implementing plans for resolving the issue.

To ensure full participation by individuals and groups that are either directly or indirectly affected by the selected issue, the college and its community-based programming management team engages in the following processual tasks.

Processual Task 7. The community college studies, analyzes, and maps the public in its service area that is affected by the issue selected for resolution.

Processual Task 8. The community college selects and uses effective processes and techniques for identifying both the formal and informal leaders within the target public and stakeholder groups.

Processual Task 9. The community college initiates dialogue with leaders of the target public and stakeholders to encourage and assist these leaders in attaining consensus on the importance of the issue and in forming a coalition to address the issue.

> **Processual Task 10.** *The community college engages the coalition in further studying and analyzing the issue, refining the definition of the issue, and deciding upon strategies to be pursued in resolving it.*

It is essential that the members of the target public be involved in defining the issue and that they agree and commit to being a part of its resolution to ensure their empowerment through the community-based programming process. Stakeholders must come to see the issue through the eyes of the target public. As they come to understand the target public's goals in relation to the issue, stakeholders collaborate with the leaders of the target public to help the target public meet those goals.

In addition, stakeholders must also be helped to realize that pooling resources is more effective than working alone. The college's community-based programming management team must work closely with the formal and the informal leaders of the target public and stakeholder groups to further study and analyze the issue and to build consensus on a collaborative plan for resolving that issue. The objective is for these leaders to commit to forming an issue-based coalition and to work toward resolution of the issue.

For example, let us suppose that a community college's environmental scanning committee has determined that one issue of importance in the community is that adults with incomes below the poverty line are suffering poor health because of improper nutrition and exercise practices. (See the illustrated plan of action in chapter 5.) Let us further suppose that the issue has been confirmed and legitimated with governing officials and other authority figures by the college's president. Then the management team's definition of the target public would include those adults below the poverty level who have been identified as neither knowing nor following recommended practices for nutrition and exercise. Stakeholders in this case would include health educators and nutritionists from health departments, the Cooperative Extension Service, and hospitals; private exercise consultants; and faculty members of colleges and universities. The college's community-based programming management team, with the assistance of community contacts, would begin the process of studying, analyzing, and mapping the target public and the stakeholders affected by this issue. By studying the issue, the target public, and the stakeholders using the processes described in this chapter, the management team would gain a greater understanding of economic, cultural, institutional, and environmental factors that are directly and indirectly linked with the target public and stakeholders. The results of this analysis might reveal financial constraints on food purchases, cultural or religious constraints on food selection, or environmental constraints on physical exercise, all of which could be contributing to the target public's poor health status.

Through dialogue with leaders of the target public and stakeholder groups, the college's community-based programming management team would then facilitate the establishment of a coalition to address the issue of poor nutritional and exercise practices among low-income adults. The coalition members would need to understand that their efforts to resolve this issue must be collaborative in nature. Since the primary change that must occur is in the food selection, preparation, and consumption habits of the target public, as well as their exercise behaviors, its members must be receptive to the changes proposed for resolving the issue. However, the target public is not the only group that needs to agree upon collaboration. For example, if resolving the issue will require the target public to change the foods its members regularly eat, health and nutrition educators must adapt the content of their programs to address any underlying cultural or financial restrictions. Stakeholders offering programs to the target public need to know the culture, social organization, and needs of the target public, including dietary practices and preferences. The stakeholders may need to adjust their way of behaving, so the target public can change. Resolving a complex issue requires a collaborative approach.

Intended Outcomes of Processual Tasks 7-10

Processual tasks 7, 8, 9, and 10 are intended to produce specific outcomes. Monitoring these outcomes (as described in chapters 5 and 6) provides an effective means for evaluating movement through the community-based programming process. Some of the outcomes to be realized when processual tasks 7, 8, 9, and 10 have been completed follow.

1. The community-based programming management team will have gained a thorough understanding of the target public and its stakeholder groups—their organization, culture, goals, and aspirations.

2. The team will have identified the formal and the informal leaders of the target public and stakeholder groups.

3. The team will have gained access to the target public and stakeholders through dialogue with their leaders; consensus will have been achieved among these leaders on the issue to be resolved; and the leaders will have committed to forming a coalition to address the issue.

4. With the assistance of the community-based programming management team, the coalition will have evolved into a collaborative team and, through further analysis of the issue, will have achieved consensus on the issue and subissues to be resolved.

The purposes of this chapter are to help present and clarify the concepts of identifying the target public, stakeholders, and leaders; identification; building consensus among the leaders about the importance of the issue; and achieving collaborative issue resolution by engaging leaders of the target public and stakeholders in studying, analyzing, and refining their understanding of the issue and deciding on strategies for resolving it. The first step is to gain an understanding of the various individuals, groups, agencies, and organizations that are directly or indirectly affected by the issue. This understanding is acquired through processual task 7.

Studying, Analyzing, and Mapping the Target Public

Processual Task 7. The community college studies, analyzes, and maps the public in its service area that is affected by the issue selected for resolution.

Study, analysis, and mapping are systematic processes for identifying and gaining an understanding of the target public affected by the issue. These processes also identify the stakeholders who have a vested interest in the issue or the welfare of the target public. These processes are conducted in relation to *one* issue, for each issue has a specific target public and particular stakeholders who must be identified. While study, analysis, and mapping may result in an actual graphic representation of the community, their primary product is a cognitive or mental map of how people are organized and how they interact with regard to a specific issue.

Study, analysis, and mapping of the target public and stakeholders for the issue are facilitated by the community-based programming management team. To help in completing this task, the management team can recruit community leaders who are knowledgeable about the issue and who can assist in acquiring a clearer understanding of the target public.

The most important outcome of the study, analysis, and mapping processes is to identify and acquire an understanding of the target public, since it is the members of that public who *must* undergo change to resolve the issue. It is important to understand and work with the target public in a manner that is compatible with its culture. For change to be meaningful and lasting, the target public must play an active role in analyzing the issue, thus gaining ownership of the change and becoming empowered by the collaborative decision-making process.

Identifying the target public, of course, is not as simple as saying, for example, "all those people who do not maintain proper diets and exercise." There may not be a natural grouping of individuals with poor health. Members of this target public may live in different parts of the service area, they may be employed in various locations, and their children may not attend the same schools. Nevertheless, there are strategies for gathering information about the target public to determine similarities and differences within the group. A comprehensive, collaborative approach to issue resolution necessitates that the management team gain an understanding of how the members of the target public are organized, what their culture is like, what their goals are, and how they define the issue.

Appropriate *conceptual tools and strategies* must be used by the community-based programming management team in the process of studying, analyzing, and mapping the target public and stakeholders. These tools and strategies can be grouped into three major categories according to their focus: social subdivisions, political subdivisions, and health and human services determinants (Boone, 1985). In examining social subdivisions, four sociological tools can be helpful to the community-based management team: social system analysis, social stratification, social differentiation, and cultural analysis.

In addition to examining social subdivisions using these sociological tools, the team will need to learn how the target public and stakeholders are organized in terms of political boundaries (such as towns and counties) and according to the health and human services available to them. This information can reveal patterns of interaction that can bind people together to achieve common goals.

The conceptual tools to be described in this section can be used in a number of ways to examine how members of the target public live, determine how they are grouped, examine their culture, and assess how they interact with one another. It is important to use a full array of methods to gain a broad understanding of the target public and stakeholders. For example, census data could be used to reveal demographics among people who have poor health due to improper nutrition. But relying on these data alone will result in an incomplete and therefore potentially inaccurate understanding of the target public. Members of the target public have many other common characteristics and goals that determine the way they interact, and an understanding of the dynamics of their interactions learned through direct interaction will reveal to the community-based programming management team specific opportunities and impediments to bringing about the changes that must occur to resolve the issue.

Sociological Tools

Social Systems Analysis. People group themselves together and develop patterns of behavior to achieve common goals; these groupings are referred to as *social systems* (Loomis, 1960). Social systems may be families, churches, neighborhoods, and even larger communities such as community college service areas, states, and nations. Both the target public and stakeholder groups can be mapped and identified using this concept of a social system. What defines a social system are the patterns of interaction that the people within that system use to attain common goals.

Examining the target public as a social system is important because this process carries the team to an understanding deeper than a simple written or visual categorization—for example, "people in poverty who do not have proper nutrition and exercise practices." Acquiring an in-depth, personal understanding of how members of the target public live their lives and what they find important is central to involving them and their leaders in resolving the issue in a manner that will be acceptable to them.

Some of the most important things to understand are the *goals and aspirations* of the target public. Members of the target public might want to be physically fit and healthy, but they also have other goals that must be understood in relation to their health and physical fitness goals. They have goals concerning use of their finances that may affect what foods they choose to buy. They may have aspirations to be as thin as possible, but the weight they seek to maintain might not be considered by experts to be healthy.

The goals of the target public do not exist in a vacuum. The community-based programming management team needs to understand the *beliefs* and *values* that underlie these goals and the ways that members of the target public attempt to reach their goals. Some individuals might believe that certain foods have nutritional values or even medicinal properties that are not supported by research. They may use examples from their own experience to support their beliefs, such as citing people who have lived long lives by eating particular foods. The strength of these beliefs must be understood by the members of the community-based programming management team if they are to develop a thorough understanding of the target public.

Quite often distrust between members of different groups arises from conflicting values. It is essential that the values of the target public be understood without attempting to impose external values on its members. People value those things that they perceive will help them achieve their goals and meet their needs. For example, homemakers who place great value on the food preferences of their family members will need to find that the dietary recommendations of educational programs are compatible with those food preferences before they will accept those recommendations. Their families must like the foods that are recommended, so they will make them part of their regular diet.

Members of the target public may have strong *feelings* or *sentiments* about people, organizations, or ways of behaving. For a health-care issue, for example, they might have strong feelings of attachment or loyalty to certain health-care providers because of good relationships developed over a period of years. They may want these preferred health-care providers to play a part in decisions about the foods they eat. Understanding these sentiments will provide ways for the community-based programming management team to communicate with the target public and develop a climate of collaboration in which the members of that public feel safe and respected.

Beliefs, knowledge, values, perceptions, and sentiments affect the way that people behave and interact within their family, church, place of work, community, or any other social system in which they hold membership. As members of a target public use certain behaviors and find these behaviors effective in achieving their goals and meeting their needs, the behaviors become accepted as the normal ways in which people should behave. These accepted ways of behaving are called *norms*. The norm for what foods are served for Sunday dinner in Christian cultures, for example, is based on a combination of beliefs, values, and sentiments concerning certain foods, family and societal traditions and preferences, and the perception of Sunday as a special day.

When behaviors have become accepted as norms, members of the social system use various methods to encourage adoption of the accepted behaviors and to discourage other behaviors. Rewards and punishments, sometimes called *sanctions,* are used to encourage acceptable patterns of behavior. The community-based programming management team needs to understand *why* certain behaviors became norms. Suppose that walking is an accepted form of exercise for people in some neighborhoods but not in the neighborhood where members of the target public live. What beliefs, values, sentiments, and sanctions have become attached to walking as an exercise in one neighborhood and not in the other? Do residents of one neighborhood punish family members for walking in the neighborhood because it is considered unsafe? The management team must know.

Different members of a social system, such as a target public, are responsible for employing various ways and means to help the social system reach its goals and meet its needs. For example, in some low-income communities, many residents do not have automobiles. However, other members of these communities who do own automobiles might take responsibility for helping others who do not have access to transportation. Offering this service designates a particular *role* for the transportation provider. Homemakers play a certain role in the community. A minister of a local church and the mayor of a town also have certain roles. Each of these roles has a status and function in the community that must be understood by the community-based programming management team. These roles and their status are a crucial part of the relationships that must be understood in order to grasp how the target public and other stakeholder groups accomplish their goals.

It is also important to understand what *facilities* or *resources* are available to the target public and the stakeholders, and especially how those resources affect the identified issue. Resources may be material, human, or financial. Directly related to assessing these resources is identifying the people in the target public and other stakeholder groups who have the *power* and *influence* to marshall the resources needed to resolve the issue. People who have access to these resources must be involved in resolving the issue.

Each family, church, agency, organization, or community has particular *patterns of communication* that define its social system and its members. A pattern of communication can be as obvious as a mailing list or as subtle as an informal "grapevine" of people in the target public who are privy to important, word-of-mouth communications. Being part of a communication channel determines who is a member of a social system and who is not. Also, some methods of communication and sources of information may be considered more acceptable than others. Consider the low-income target public used as an example for the nutrition and exercise issue. In publicizing programs designed to address the issue, it would be necessary to know whether members of the target public would respond better to programs promoted through the local church or by certain leaders in neighborhoods than to announcements placed in the newspaper.

Each social system also has accepted ways of instructing new members in normal behaviors and old members in new behaviors. This "instruction" process is referred to as *socialization*. Suppose that a target public's processes for socializing its members in dietary practices is matriarchal, being carried out by mothers and grandmothers. The target public might find that learning about good nutrition through the school or workplace conflicts with this traditional way of learning what foods to eat and how to prepare them. In other cases, members of a target public may find their beliefs compatible with an agency's educational programs.

When members of the social system accept new behaviors, beliefs, or values, these new ideas begin to become *institutionalized*. Institutionalization of new behaviors and values is critical to success in bringing about long-term change in the target public's behavior. In addressing the issue of nutrition practices among a target public, improved eating practices must become institutionalized behaviors and values of the family, church, and school if they are to have a lasting effect within the target public. Institutionalizing the new behaviors and values might mean that the new foods are accepted in families' regular diets, that they are accepted at social and religious gatherings, and that they are included on school lunch menus.

A social system maintains *social control* over the accepted behaviors of its members. A target public may be subject to the laws of a state or nation that has social controls, such as laws that govern how food must be processed and advertised. But those same means of social control may not have complete power within the *boundaries* of the particular community in which the target public lives. The community has processes for boundary maintenance that protect its identity and its survival. If the target public lives in a rural community, its members may have loyalties to local farmers who sell their produce directly to the target public. The community maintains its identity, protects its farmers, and possibly holds food prices down by maintaining this boundary that distinguishes community members from others. Boundary maintenance is also evident among many of the agencies that are stakeholders in an issue. In this case, the process is often referred to as *turf protection.*

Social systems may also be defined by their connections to other social systems. These connections are called *systemic linkages.* Using stakeholders as an example, linkages may exist between a local health department and public schools, boards of county commissioners, and hospitals that help to define how its health educators operate. The health department also has ties to parent organizations such as a state board of health and the state legislature; these linkages also help define how the health department exists and operates. A target public, on the other hand, will have linkages to its churches, its schools, and other institutions that serve its needs.

Analysis of Social Stratification and Social Differentiation. Two tools that can be used to examine a target public as a social system are *social stratification* and *social differentiation. Social stratification* is the general ordering of people into social classes according to their level of income, occupational status, level of education, and cultural heritage. *Social differ-*

entiation is a process of sorting people out by shared characteristics within these social classes. Quite often the demographic data used to describe a target public represent information about either social stratification or social differentiation. People are sometimes grouped (or group themselves) according to commonalities in their socioeconomic status or their cultural heritage. Regardless of whether social stratification rankings are perceived as having positive or negative effects on the quality of life for the community, they always affect how people form groups to meet their needs and achieve their goals. Some issues affect only certain "classes," whereas other issues cut across class boundaries. In working with these groups, the community college's community-based programming team must understand how these classes protect their boundaries or seek alliances with other groups to maintain or improve their security or status.

Social differentiation is usually determined by such characteristics as gender, age, marital status, and size of family but may also be determined by education and occupation. Social differentiation enables us to understand the differences among members within a social system or social strata. These differences may reveal smaller groups, or subsystems, that share common goals and life-styles. Families with children may have very different life-styles from single adults in regard to their eating and nutrition practices. Older people may have different dietary needs than middle-aged or younger adults.

Using social differentiation as a tool for studying subgroups of people within the target public involves more than just analyzing quantitative data and written documents. Gaining real understanding requires interacting with people about the issue, their aspirations, and their everyday lives. The analysis process results in understanding how people live and interact and helps the community-based programming team develop a thorough understanding of the target public and stakeholders on an issue.

Cultural Analysis. Another sociological tool that is useful in the study, analysis, and mapping of target publics and stakeholders is the analysis of their *cultures*. Culture is the way of life of a definable grouping of people, such as a target public. Just as social systems are made up of subsystems, there are subcultures within cultures. While social system concepts help us to understand how people are organized and interact, analysis of culture leads to an understanding of the collective behavior of systems. A culture includes all the learned and expected ways of life within a society as well as the artifacts, buildings, tools, and other physical objects in the environment that are shared by members of that society.

Just as the concept of culture is not easily understood, learning about a specific culture is probably the most difficult—yet most important—task in studying groups, communities, organizations, and other social systems. Culture cannot be reduced to any one norm, value, or artifact of a society. It is the sum of all things learned and created by that society. Understanding a culture as a whole provides a way, in turn, of analyzing each norm, value, or artifact. The consumption of fatty meats, for example, can be viewed differently depending on the culture being examined. Limiting the intake of such meat in a culture where it is viewed as just one of many available foods may be easier than in a culture where it is considered a delicacy. In the latter culture, this type of meat and its proper preparation may be a tradition that has been passed down through generations of cooks. The availability of fatty meats may be seen as a symbol of prosperity in the face of scarce resources.

For the target public and stakeholder groups to work together to resolve issues of common concern, it is important that the community-based programming management team begin to understand the different cultures of those groups. Equally important is that the groups come to understand each other's cultures. One does not have to look far to find examples of the importance of such understanding. The culture of American businesses, for example, centers on supplying a product or service for profit. The cultures of social service and educational institutions, on the other hand, focus on solving problems through non-profit, cost-effective resources and learning experiences. When an issue includes business, service, and educational organizations among the stakeholder groups, conflict between approaches to resolving the issue might occur because members of each group may not recognize that they are conforming to their own culture's learned patterns of behavior rather than looking for new, collaborative approaches. Consider, for example, a proposal to implement an exercise program at an industry site. A recreation department might have difficulty communicating to site managers how this program can benefit employees if the department does not also take into account how it may help increase the industry's profit through improved employee health. A private fitness center seeking a contract to offer these programs might already be in tune with this profit-making approach of both the parties involved. Sensitivity to the potential for conflict across cultures may help the community-based programming management team to present issues in terms that embrace different cultures or express the issue in neutral terms that minimize the likelihood of conflict.

Just as there are subsystems within larger social systems, there are sub-cultures within larger cultures, and these, too, can find themselves in conflict when attempting to resolve an issue. Quite often the things that are shared and learned in the larger culture find expression in subtly different ways among the subsystems' cultures. For example, all subsystems of a larger target public system may believe that elderly and disabled citizens should receive adequate health care. However, one subsystem's culture may favor responses that provide for care in the home, while another subsystem's culture may support care in nursing home facilities. Yet another may favor the support of extended families. Each of these responses represents a sum of that subsystem's cultural values, beliefs, resources, heritage, and ways of life. These differences might be found between urban and rural neighborhoods, between extended family systems versus those that have become more independent or isolated, or between groups that lack the resources needed to obtain quality in-home care and those that have such resources.

Analysis of Political Subdivisions

Analysis of political subdivisions, a tool commonly employed by program planners, can be used to map the target public. As the community college's community-based programming management team begins to understand where members of the target public are located in the service area, they will observe individuals interacting with each other as members of particular municipalities, counties, neighborhoods, voting districts, or other areas, which are often referred to as *political subdivisions*. These subdivisions, of course, provide helpful understanding of how people are grouped according to common interests dictated by geographic proximity or by the power structures of a larger area, such as a state or nation. By virtue of the political structures of these subdivisions, people share common values, goals, and concerns. Often, formally or informally assigned roles make the political functions of the subdivision work. Members of a target public will live in and be affected by a number of political subdivisions. Political subdivisions are often represented by an organized group or official body of leaders charged with concern for the quality of life in the community and having some degree of control over the resources within its boundaries. These bodies might be neighborhood associations, town councils, or boards of commissioners. A thorough understanding of the target public requires knowing who wields real influence and power within these political subdivisions.

Analysis of Health and Human Services Determinants

A target public will also include members of a population who use certain *health and human services,* such as hospitals, schools, businesses, or employers because of their geographic location or population density. Use of these services creates connections among members of the target public. Health and human services are influenced by and have influence on how people group themselves and develop patterns of interaction to meet their needs. Basic health and human service systems generally include those pertaining to education, commerce, religion, and health.

The availability of certain natural resources, products, or services can help to determine whether industries, businesses, or even educational facilities choose to locate in an area. Population density may determine whether a central shopping area or neighborhood shopping centers are built. Combined with personal preferences, population density may have an effect on the number of churches in an area. The presence of a large river or lake in the area may determine where people live and how they are employed—for example, at a hydroelectric plant or in the tourism and recreation industry.

The use of the conceptual tools previously described in this chapter will enable the community-based programming team to develop a thorough understanding of who the target public and stakeholders are, how they are organized, and how they are linked and related to one another. This understanding is critical to gaining the involvement of the target public and stakeholders in resolution of the issue. Community-based programming cannot be carried out by imposing an externally created plan on the target public; on the contrary, community-based programming is a planned program systematically developed through identification of and collaboration with the target public and its stakeholder groups. The study, analysis, and mapping of the target public and stakeholders result in an understanding of the cultural, social, political, and institutional context within which the target public and stakeholders exist. Incorporation of this information into the community-based programming process is essential to the successful resolution of the identified issue.

As stated, inclusion of the target public and stakeholders in the planning process is critical. However, it is usually unrealistic to have every member of the target public and the stakeholder groups involved in this collaborative process. Therefore, formal and informal leaders of these groups must be identified and encouraged to commit to working together to resolve the identified issue. Processual task 8 pertains to identifying these leaders.

Identifying Formal and Informal Leaders

Processual Task 8. *The community college selects and uses effective processes and techniques for identifying both the formal and the informal leaders within the target public and stakeholder groups.*

The key to accessing and involving the target public in resolving the issue is gaining the commitment and support of its formal and informal leaders. The leaders of the target public are able to represent their culture and its concerns about the issue, and they also have influence with members of the target public (Boone, 1985). This representation and influence is essential to gaining access to the target public and involving its members in bringing about the changes necessary to resolve the issue. The target public's leaders will work for those changes in their system that they perceive as beneficial to the people they represent. Also important is identifying the leaders of the stakeholder groups that can legitimately represent and influence their agency's or organization's involvement in resolution of the issue. The community college's community-based programming management team must be skilled in applying concepts, such as *formal and informal leaders* and *leader identification approaches,* that help in identifying leaders who are recognized and supported by the target public and the stakeholders.

Leaders can be divided into two major types: *formal leaders* and *informal leaders*. It is important to understand how these leaders can be characterized and how they represent the target public or stakeholder group. Formal leaders are those highly visible persons who are recognized and accepted in leadership roles. The term is applied to people who have become leaders by virtue of position, reputation, social participation, or their reputation for making the "right" decisions. These are often the people that we seek out because they control needed resources. Informal leaders are those persons who are not highly visible to the members of the group they represent but who nonetheless wield considerable influence on the behavior and actions of that group. These are the people that we seek to involve in programs because by virtue of their accomplishments, heritage, and intimacy with the target public or stakeholders, they have highly valued opinions. Therefore, they are often "gatekeepers" or guardians of the values, customs, and beliefs of those groups. Several approaches can be used to identify formal and informal leaders of the target public and stakeholder groups. The following sections present some of these approaches (Bell, Hill, & Wright, 1961); each represents a different aspect of leadership that is important to understand.

Positional Approach

It is relatively easy to identify persons who occupy formal positions of leadership in the target public or stakeholder group when they are in highly visible positions. For example, individuals in such positions as minister, rabbi, mayor, public agency director, business owner, voluntary organization director, and union head may be readily identified. These leaders usually wield influence over the resources of the group or organization they represent.

Social Participation Approach

The extent of a person's participation in the activities of voluntary and community organizations can sometimes be a good indicator of leadership. By this approach, the people who join or participate in the most organizations are identified as leaders. These leaders may be excellent sources of information about the culture and organization of the target public. However, the specific activities must be examined to determine the amount (if any) of power and influence that these leaders wield among target publics or stakeholders. The "joiner" may be a good source of information but may not be able to mobilize resources or influence behaviors of the organizations in which he or she serves.

For example, suppose that a member of a target public is very active as a Meals-on-Wheels volunteer and is also a member and attends meetings of the American Association for Retired Persons, the National Alzheimer's Association, and the local elder-care provider organization. This person might be considered a leader, but he or she may or may not have any power to affect the community's public decisions about providing for the health of its citizens. The person's interest may stem from personal responsibilities in caring for elderly relatives, or the person may be an emerging leader who does not yet have a great deal of influence with the target public of which she or he is a member. However, the person may be very knowledgeable and helpful in identifying other leaders of the target public. In other cases, the person may be very active in a number of organizations *and* have power and influence with the target public.

Reputational Approach

Members of a group can also be identified as leaders by the extent to which others within the group regard them as leaders. In this approach, members of a group are asked to tell who they think their most influential leaders are—in other words, which members have the reputation of being leaders for that group. Those leaders that are mentioned most often are considered the reputational leaders.

For example, the formal leadership of organizations indigenous to the target public, such as churches, neighborhood associations, and Cooperative Extension Service homemaker clubs, might be asked to identify the three people they consider to be the most influential in the lives of the people in the community and in decisions concerning a health issue. This process might begin with asking knowledgeable contacts in the community to identify those persons among the target public who have the reputation of being influential with its members. The leaders who are identified might then be asked to identify who they think other reputational leaders are. The interviews would generate a list of names. It is important to keep track of how many times each leader is identified. For instance, eight leaders might have been identified by 75 percent of the people interviewed. It could be assumed that the majority of the target public recognizes these eight leaders by their reputation.

Decision-Making Approach

Although similar to the reputational approach, the decision-making approach differs in that actual involvement in making public decisions is the basis for identifying leaders. The method is applied by investigating one or more specific policy decisions to identify the individuals who influenced the decision. Using the nutrition and exercise issue as an example, let us assume that members of the target public were involved in establishing an additional health educator position in a county. Establishing this position might have required a number of public meetings with the agency that would house the health educator and with governing bodies that would fund the position. Establishing the position would require that a number of key decisions be made. A careful review of the minutes of meetings and holding conversations with those involved in the meetings can disclose untapped leadership among people concerned about the issue and who had some form of power and influence over the outcome.

Opinion-Leadership Approach

To identify opinion leaders, members of a group are asked to name those persons from whom they would ask advice on a topic of concern. The persons identified most often may be regarded as the opinion leaders on that topic. This approach can reveal the leaders who help to shape the opinions of a target public with respect to the issue being addressed.

Consider an example of how the opinion-leadership approach might be used by a community-based programming management team addressing the issue of access to health care. Suppose that some of the more experienced members of low-skill labor unions (which have been previously identified as associated with the health-care issue) are asked who they trust to help them make decisions about efforts to improve their access to health care. One element of this access might be making use of the medical insurance programs provided through the union. The names most often identified for each of the unions are recorded. Some of these persons might be members who had been successful in coping with difficult situations concerning their own families' health and who had then helped others by sharing what they learned from the experience. It is important to remember that this approach is different from the reputational approach. In the reputational approach, the identified leaders have influence with a variety of public or other policy decisions that affect the target public, but especially in health-care issues. The opinion-leadership approach, on the other hand, is specific to the issue and reveals leaders who not only may affect policy decisions but who also affect the daily lives of people in the community. These people may often comprise the grassroots leadership of a community, leadership that is seldom directly involved in issue resolution but that has effective connections within the target public.

It is important to understand the type of power or influence that a person has within his or her social system—formal or informal, social, political, or religious. The type will determine the approach needed to obtain that person's involvement in resolving the issue. Once leaders have been identified, they must be invited to discuss the issue, the needs and interests of the target public and stakeholders, and the fundamental need for broad-based collaboration to resolve the issue. A key responsibility of the community-based programming management team is to establish a dialogue with these leaders to confirm the importance of the issue and gain their commitment to collaborative action. Processual task 9 describes this process.

Reaching Consensus on the Issue and Forming a Coalition to Resolve It

Processual Task 9. The community college initiates dialogue with leaders of the target public and stakeholders to encourage and assist these leaders in attaining consensus on the importance of the issue and in forming a coalition to address the issue.

Identifying the leaders of the target public and stakeholder groups is critical, and equally important is the need for the community-based programming management team to develop an awareness among these leaders of how the issue is affecting the quality of life for members of the target public. Cultivating this awareness among the leaders opens the door for developing consensus that the issue is important to the well-being of the target public and for developing agreement that it needs to be resolved. The desired outcome for processual task 9 is for the leaders of the target public and stakeholders to achieve consensus on the issue to be resolved and to commit to collaborative resolution of the issue through formation of a coalition.

Listening Skills

To develop this consensus on the issue and commitment to forming a coalition, the members of the community-based programming management team must possess and apply communication skills to establish positive interaction with the leaders of the target public and stakeholder groups. The management team must develop informal and formal relationships with the leaders of the target public and stakeholder groups, relationships that will focus their attention on the importance of resolving the issue through collaboration. Fostering an atmosphere of collaboration and consensus demands that trusting relationships be developed among target public and stakeholder leaders and the community-based programming management team. The most basic interpersonal skill needed in developing the relationship is that of *listening.* Boone, Dolan, and Shearon (1971) suggest

The identification of the leaders of their public by change agents is not sufficient; rather, they must consciously strive to establish communication with these persons through informal and meaningful dialogue. The dialogue should be characterized with the familiar as perceived by the leaders. That is, the inputs of the leaders into such conversation(s) should be dominant. The change agent is characterized as a listener in the initial stages of such dialogue. The professional should strive to exhibit as much empathy as possible. Only after a "positive" two-way relationship is established should the change agent begin to interject external information into the dialogue. Such dialogue should not be restricted to a single encounter, but ideally should be considered through the period of time required to establish a meaningful and continuing relationship between the adult educator and his public(s) (p. 9).

Through listening, the community-based programming management team will learn what is important to the leaders of the target public and stakeholders concerning the issue and will discover how the culture of the target public and of the stakeholder groups influences what these leaders see as important. In addition, the leaders of the target public and stakeholder groups will have the opportunity to learn about each other, understand the ways in which their needs and goals are compatible, and understand the areas in which they will need to collaborate to find strategies and solutions that are acceptable to all.

Also through listening, the management team members can help build consensus among the leaders of the target public and stakeholders as to the importance of the issue to the quality of life for the target public and to acquire a commitment from the leaders to form a coalition for collaborative resolution of the issue. An understanding of what collaboration is and the need for collaborative responses to issues will help the management team member as he or she seeks this consensus through dialogue.

Collaboration and Commitment to Forming the Coalition

Collaboration means that leaders of the target public and stakeholders engage jointly and equally in working toward resolution of an issue:

> *To collaborate is to work jointly with significant others in seeking solutions to an issue...implicit in collaboration is mutual agreement by those involved on the definition and nature of the issue, goals to be pursued in resolving the issue, and a plan of action for resolving the issue (Boone, 1992, p. 3).*

This collaboration has been referred to as the "creation of a unified synergy that transcends the forces of fragmentation in the community and cultivates a cooperative spirit of teamwork, resolve, and optimism among the people, their leaders, and stakeholder groups and organizations" (Boone, 1992, p. 3). Various leaders who represent the target public and stakeholders are brought together to collaborate as equals in their vision, mission, and commitment. Consensus, or the process of arriving at a decision with the support of all those affected by that decision, is an integral part of collaboration.

According to Gray (1989), collaboration provides a method by which individuals, groups, and organizations can constructively manage their differences. In applying Gray's concepts to community-based programming, the college's management team helps the leaders of the target public and stakeholder groups recognize the potential advantages of working together toward a common goal.

Gray describes collaboration as a process of joint decision making among the target public and other stakeholders that is characterized by the following: (1) the target public and other stakeholders are interdependent; (2) solutions emerge by dealing constructively with differences; (3) joint ownership of decisions is involved; (4) the target public and other stakeholders assume collective responsibility for the future direction of the issue; and (5) collaboration is an emergent, or ongoing, process. It is this atmosphere for joint decision making to which the leaders of the target public and stakeholders will need to commit.

Thus, assembling representative leaders of the target public and stakeholders to work out an agreement among themselves represents the initial phase in the development of a coalition. As leaders of the target public and stakeholders consider becoming part of the coalition, they must believe that it will involve work to be conducted jointly and on an equal power basis for the resolution of an issue of common concern. As such, collaboration must be perceived by these coalition leaders as a process through which parties who see different aspects of a problem can constructively explore their differences and search for solutions that go beyond their own limited vision of what is possible (Gray, 1989). Collaboration must be seen as nonadversarial.

Members of the community-based programming management team engage in dialogue with leaders of the target public and stakeholders, and through listening and asking questions they come to understand the culture and concerns of these leaders. This trusting relationship and the expectation for a nonadversarial, collaborative approach to issue resolution are necessary conditions to gaining the commitment of the leaders of the target public and stakeholders to form a coalition.

Formation of a Coalition

Arising from the informal relationships developed with the leaders of the target public and stakeholders, a formal coalition begins to take shape. This coalition is a temporary organization comprising leaders of the target public and stakeholder groups formed to seek resolution of an issue. Formation of a coalition is a critical stage in the community-based programming process, because it represents the transition of responsibility for issue identification and resolution from the community college to the target public and stakeholders. Henceforth, the coalition has responsibility for resolving of the issue. The community college moves into the role of facilitator and acts as a resource to the coalition.

The coalition is the embodiment of the philosophies that are at the heart of community-based programming: collaboration, inclusiveness, two-way communication, and a one-to-one power ratio. The effective formation of the coalition and its engagement in addressing a specific issue are the most critical steps in the community-based programming process. The coalition's members have been identified as leaders of groups that must participate in specific changes or must provide resources for those changes if the issue is to be resolved. Their task as coalition members is to work together—collaborate—to resolve the issue.

Successfully convening the first meeting of the coalition depends upon developing consensus on the importance of the issue and commitment to collaborative resolution by and among the target public, stakeholders, and their leaders. Through knowledge and understanding of the culture and concerns of these leaders, the convener (the community college or its community-based programming management team) will know how to approach the potential members and encourage them to participate in the coalition. If previous processual tasks have been completed successfully, potential concerns such as turf protection and power balance will have already been recognized through informal discussions, and the commitment of the leaders to take collaborative action on the issue will have already been gained. When letters or telephone calls announce the date of the first coalition meeting, leaders will have already committed to collaborative participation.

The coalition formed as a result of building consensus and commitment is a new group of leaders, representing the target public and other stakeholders, who may not have worked together previously. The characteristics of the leaders and the target public's culture, as represented by its leaders, must be understood when developing meaningful relationships within this group.

However, the purpose of forming the coalition is broader than informing the target public and stakeholder groups about each other's cultures, needs, and goals. The coalition will work on further refining the definition of the specified issue, will identify the subissues that must be considered, and will reach consensus on the strategies that must be used to resolve the issue. During that process, the college's community-based management team will facilitate the coalition's study of the identified issue. This process is further elaborated in processual task 10.

Clarifying the Issue and Developing Strategies

Processual Task 10. The community college engages the coalition in further studying and analyzing the issue, refining the definition of the issue, and deciding upon strategies to be pursued in resolving it.

As the college and its community-based programming management team engage in processual task 10, the coalition formed from the leaders of the target public and stakeholder groups are meeting face-to-face. The management team takes on the roles of convener and facilitator as it brings the coalition together and engages it in addressing the issue.

The initial task for the coalition members is to reach consensus on a more focused definition of the issue and the strategies to be used in the issue's resolution. Up to this point, the issue has been defined in broad or "macro" terms. The coalition's first task is to collaboratively study, analyze, and refine their definition of the macro issue by examining the economic, social-cultural, political, and technological forces affecting the macro issue and the target public. Through this process, more manageable subissues that are part of the larger issue are identified. It is important that all of the efforts be tied to the advancement of a shared vision by the coalition members. While the primary outcome for processual task 10 is a coalition that has collaboratively made the critical decisions that will be translated into a plan of action, the coalition must become more than just an aggregate of leaders of the target public and stakeholders. It is through shared refinement of the issue's definition and reaching a shared vision of the resolution of the issue that plans for collaborative resolution of the issue can be developed. And it is this kind of collaboration that must characterize the coalition and how it does its work.

To assist the coalition in accomplishing these tasks while further developing its collaborative nature, the community-based programming management team must understand and be skilled in using such concepts as *collaboration* (specifically applied to engaging the coalition); *group development; team building; communication skills; conflict resolution; study, analysis, and refinement of the issue; and vision,* including the relationship of vision to goals and the strategies for resolution of the issue.

Collaboration is needed to develop and maintain the desired productive climate in the coalition and to develop a thorough understanding of the issue and its subissues. The following section discusses the concept of collaboration and the skills needed to apply it to decisions made by the coalition.

Collaboration in the Coalition

Collaboration and shared visions are intended to advance the collective good of the target public and stakeholders involved (Gray, 1989). Successfully advancing a shared vision requires identification and involvement of the target public and a diverse set of stakeholders, each of whom holds some but not all of the necessary resources for issue resolution. To continue using as an example the issue of proper nutrition and exercise, suppose that a neighborhood church is an important stakeholder with a role to play in providing resources for resolution of the issue. Will the church, by being a player in the collaborative process, see the spiritual rewards that might be gained by attending to the physical needs of its community members? Can its leaders and members share a common vision with health educators? This common vision must be achieved if they are to work collaboratively on resolving the issue.

Collaboration within the coalition is not just cooperation. *Cooperation* entails forming partnerships and agreements to work together to meet goals, but it does not substantially change the services provided or the rules and regulations governing the separateness of cooperating institutions, individuals, or groups (Melaville & Bland, 1993). Cooperation alone usually does not result in the building of a coalition.

Collaboration in the coalition is also more than coordination. *Coordination* refers to formal, institutionalized relationships among the existing networks of organizations (Mulford, 1984). To presume that the target public or stakeholders in a collaborative effort are already part of an organized relationship minimizes the developmental character of the collaborative process. An industry may cooperate by sending workers to a training program, or it may coordinate with the community college by providing class space after work hours. These actions can occur without the kind of collaboration that might occur when the industry adopts released-time policies and supports a nearby child-care center that adjusts its time schedules to help workers take advantage of classes. Decisions made in a coalition about refining the definition of the issue, setting goals for its resolution, and selecting strategies for reaching those goals must encompass these elements of collaboration if the coalition members are to act in concert and sustain that action until the issue has been resolved.

Group Development in the Coalition

As the coalition is making decisions about its definition of the issue, the goals it will set, and strategies for resolving the issue, it will be experiencing the group development dynamics common to the formation and operation of all groups. Although coalitions vary in terms of how much time they spend on task behavior (making decisions and planning action) and on socio-emotional behavior (managing tensions, building friendships, and being mutually supportive), they tend to make decisions collaboratively by moving through a process of gathering and sharing information, debating the merits of suggestions, accommodating differences within the group, and readjusting to the group. The community-based programming management team can facilitate movement through these stages by understanding the phases of group process.

Group Phases. Groups such as coalitions tend to develop in the sequential phases that Tuchman and Jensen (1977) call *forming, storming, norming, performing,* and *transforming.* A knowledge of group phases and what to expect in each can greatly facilitate group work. (See *Working With Our Publics,* 1989, module 5, pp. 15–22, for a more complete discussion of the Tuchman-Jensen model.) For continuity in presentation, all five stages are reviewed in this chapter, but the performing and transforming stages apply to processual tasks 11 through 15 as well.

At the *forming* stage, the coalition members get acquainted, define their roles, select a decision-making method, construct agendas, and set goals. Members of the community-based programming management team who have brought the coalition together act as its first facilitators. Uncertainty is a problem for the group at this initial stage. When a group is forming, members cautiously explore the boundaries of acceptable group behavior. The coalition may begin its work by letting the leaders of the target public and stakeholders introduce themselves, setting some rules for how members will interact (such as not allowing "put downs"), and reacting to and adjusting decision-making processes proposed by the facilitators.

Storming is characterized by Kuhn (1982) as "essential tension." In this phase the members of the coalition are asked to present their perspectives on an issue, factors affecting the issue, and possible strategies for resolving the issue. During this process of study and analysis, conflict may occur. The community-based programming management team should reassure coalition members that disagreements are normal and that expressing differences may actually benefit the coalition. The most important contribution that brainstorming makes to problem solving is idea generation. Generating ideas about the issue and the forces affecting it—distinct from deciding on solutions at this point—is the key to group creativity. The assumption is that structured brainstorming within a group produces more and better ideas than people working alone.

Norming implies that a collection of people have formed themselves into a functioning group (a coalition). As discussed earlier in this chapter, norms are informal rules that regulate group behavior (Feldman & Arnold, 1983). Norming is used to reduce differences among coalition members and to encourage the development of the group's identity by establishing common values and goals. In the case of a coalition formed to resolve an issue, the coalition moves during the norming phase from study and analysis of the issue to agreeing on a common understanding (a refined definition) of the issue, a common vision or goal that addresses the issue, and common strategies for its resolution. The coalition may need to use some of the problem-solving tools identified at the end of this chapter to facilitate reaching these decisions. (Since agreement on a formal plan of action would also constitute a norm of the coalition, moving through this stage of development actually brings the coalition into processual task 11, as described in chapter 5.) One danger in norming is the tendency for "groupthink" to occur; in groupthink, cooperation and "getting along" with each other become more important than creative thinking and the expression of individual misgivings and doubts. The result can be less than optimum decisions.

Although *performing* occurs after coalition resources have been fully mobilized to achieve a goal, as described in discussing processual task 12 in chapter 5, it will be helpful to touch briefly on this phase now in order to provide a complete understanding of how the Tuchman-Jensen phases apply to engaging the coalition in its work. By the time that the performing phase has been reached, the plan of action, described in chapter 5, has been agreed upon and the coalition begins its implementation of that plan. Effective performance at this phase depends on the amount of collaboration and consensus-building that occurred as the coalition came to agreement on the issue and on goals and strategies for its resolution. At this implementation stage of group work, coalition members have become interdependent, and they "get down to business." Leaders delegate responsibilities and empower others. "Footdragging," a tool of the uncommitted and powerless, can be a problem. Poor follow-through can also hinder progress; it is sometimes caused by a shortage of "doers" or by a lack of members' sense of ownership in the plan. These potential problems are best recognized and averted before they occur.

Groups and coalitions inevitably reach a point of *transforming,* as will be discussed in chapter 6. They may revert to earlier phases. The coalition may actually have to revisit its definition of the issue and its decisions about the goals and strategies for issue resolution. The coalition may regroup because of changes in the issue or because it perceives a need to tackle a new task, or it may simply disband after accomplishing its task (resolution of the issue).

Communication Within an Effective Coalition

Understanding the development of the coalition as a team is important to fostering the collaborative functioning of the coalition. In addition, an understanding of communication among coalition members is important because sound and open communication is critical to making good decisions about the issue and determining goals and strategies for its resolution. The requirements for effective collaboration and communication expressed in the literature on team development apply to coalitions as well.

Scholtes (1988) and Katzenbach and Smith (1993) offer suggestions for successful teams that are also applicable to coalitions. One suggestion is to ensure that members use good communication skills. Effective and productive discussions depend on how well information is passed among team members. Failure to communicate is the chief reason for conflict. Members of the community-based programming management team, acting as facilitators of the coalition, and eventually the coalition members as well, must have or develop good communication skills. They need to exhibit the characteristics of assertive communication, such as knowing when to talk, when to listen, and how to assert their needs and limits. They need to be fair, tolerant, and nonjudgmental communicators, and they must know how to work with and involve in positive ways those members who are whiners, moralizers, labelers, silents, and attackers (those who demonstrate passive or aggressive communication behaviors). They also will need to know the power of constructive confrontation—that period of communication in which a person "takes the heat of criticism."

Good communication skills mean that coalition members must listen actively, exploring rather than debating another speaker's ideas; they must know or learn how to use open questions, encouraging statements, and reflecting comments. As the coalition meets and progresses through its development as a team and discusses the decisions it must make, the community-based programming management team can help coalition members develop these communication skills. The coalition will need to develop an atmosphere in which members avoid interrupting and talking when others are speaking. Developing skills such as learning to avoid "why" questions, which tend to discourage positive communication by implying criticism or judgment, will be helpful. Beneficial team behavior means that coalition members will learn to

■ initiate discussions,

■ seek information and opinions,

■ suggest procedures for reaching a goal,

■ clarify or elaborate on ideas,

■ summarize,

■ test for consensus,

■ direct conversational traffic,

■ make room for reserved talkers,

- keep the discussion from digressing,
- note the hidden agendas,
- compromise,
- relieve tension,
- refer to external sources of information,
- praise and correct others equally, and
- get the group to agree on standards.

Resolving Conflict in the Coalition

The community-based programming team will also need conflict resolution skills to facilitate the work of the coalition. Conflict of some degree is rarely avoidable in groups and especially within coalitions. People have different needs, interests, and values; their goals and activities may be—or may seem to be—incompatible. As the coalition initially meets to study, analyze, and redefine the issue and to decide on strategies for its resolution, there is potential for conflict. Conflicts in coalitions may relate to many issues such as resources, ideas, turf, race, ethnicity, and life-style values and norms.

In community-based programming, where interdependence among a target public and stakeholders is necessary to resolve a community issue, turf struggles may occur. Stakeholders may discover that their existing programs are in conflict with the life-style and culture of the target public. Conflicts may also surface among stakeholders. For example, it is not unusual for each city and county to have a number of agencies and private organizations whose function is to deal with health, nutrition, and exercise. Some of the agencies may be well funded; some may provide a peripheral service for health care and education; and some may be very unstable. To resolve the issue, the target public and these stakeholder organizations must collaborate, even when they may want to protect their own territory.

Positive conflict can help to bring about needed change, enable people to be creative, and bring people together. If consensus is to be reached on the issue and on the goals and strategies for its resolution, the conflict experienced by a coalition must have these positive characteristics.

Negative conflict, on the other hand, is destructive. The challenge for a coalition is to resolve conflict in a constructive way. Over the last several decades, a quiet revolution has been taking place in the methods used to respond to conflict (Canfield, 1992). Win-win negotiation and mediation, in which both parties to a conflict gain some benefit, is preferred over win-lose negotiation and litigation. The win-win approach is essential to developing collaborative responses to an issue by a coalition when conflict rather than agreement occurs in discussing the issue and possible responses to it. Several terms are used to describe the various conflict resolution techniques; one such term is *negotiation,* which is direct, two-way communication between or among the people involved in a disagreement with the intention of reaching agreement. The objective of *collaborative, or win-win, negotiation* is to help all parties meet their needs by focusing on underlying interests and developing mutually beneficial alternatives. In *mediation,* a neutral third party assists the disputing parties in reaching agreement. *Arbitration* is similar to mediation, but an arbitrator determines the facts in a dispute and recommends a solution. It is helpful for members of the community-based programming management team to understand these approaches to conflict resolution, so they can help coalition members decide which approach is preferable in a particular conflict situation.

Among groups such as coalitions whose purpose is to work toward common goals, negotiation, collaboration, mediation, and sometimes arbitration are the preferred methods of resolving conflicts. *Competition,* which leads to a win-lose outcome, is considered an undesirable dispute resolution technique. A facilitator who attempts to resolve conflict within a coalition has two major tasks: *probing* (examining beneath the surface to discover and determine the real issues and identify the issues that are in conflict) and *generating solutions* (suggesting options that may meet the needs of the parties).

Probing allows the facilitator to examine negative feelings usually expressed by anger, hostility, or both. Negative feelings that are expressed and accepted often lose their strength. In the coalition, a facilitator's responses must be nondefensive, even when anger is directed at him or her. The coalition's facilitator may want to defuse the situation by engaging the angry person in a private session, thus giving the person the opportunity to express her or his anger in a nonthreatening environment. Probing beneath the surface of anger makes it possible to identify the concerns and needs of the individuals involved or the groups (target public and stakeholders) that they represent. People in conflict need to tell their story. By listening to each others' concerns, the coalition members can identify values that they hold in common about an issue or strategies for its resolution. Finally, those who are in conflict can clarify the real problem, separate it from their anger, and turn to expressions of their own needs, concerns, and values as a basis for coming to agreement.

Generating solutions is the opposite of probing. It is exploratory and open-ended. Problem solving begins with a wide-ranging exploration of all the potential options. It is focused on the present or the future, not the past. Fisher and Ury (1981) suggest moving away from personal blame and instead generating objective criteria such as precedent, scientific judgment, and specified procedures. This is what makes careful study, analysis, refinement of the issue, and development of a shared vision of the goals for resolution so important to generating options and reaching agreement on the strategies for issue resolution. All coalition members should feel that they have "won" because if any members feel that they have lost, the likelihood is that they will not fully participate in resolving the issue. One suggestion for generating solutions is *bridging common interests.* Finding out how each coalition member's interests can be met may seem difficult, but a facilitator, such as a member of the community-based programming management team, can accomplish this task. The concept of *log-rolling,* borrowed from politics, offers one way of generating ideas. Each person gives up something of lesser value in order to help each other get something of greater value. Finally, *compromise* cannot be ruled out as a way of resolving disputes.

The effective application of the group process, communication, and interpersonal skills described in the foregoing sections will help the coalition members collaborate and reach consensus as they undertake the work of processual task 10, namely, studying and analyzing the issue and refining its definition from the perspective of the target public.

Study, Analysis, and Refinement of the Issue

The further study and analysis of the issue and refinement of its definition require identifying, collecting, and sharing information and using concepts and skills described previously in this chapter to ensure that the analysis is conducted in a collaborative manner. Continuous evaluation of the decisions made by the coalition members as they study and analyze the issue is necessary to ensure that collaboration is taking place. As new information surfaces or is shared, coalition members may change their perspective on elements of the issue and therefore adjust their definition of the issue. When they reach a consensus on the particulars of the issue—in other words, when everyone agrees to support a description of the issue as generated by the coalition members—the community-based programming management team can assist the coalition in developing the statement of the issue that will be included in the plan of action. The statement of the issue concisely identifies and describes briefly the *major factors surrounding the issue, who is affected, and the subissues* encompassed in the larger macro issue. (See chapter 5 for a more detailed description of the plan of action and the statement of the issue.)

The coalition members must obtain and assess information that will help them come to consensus on the *major factors surrounding the issue.* Their analysis of the issue builds upon the work conducted by the environmental scanning committee when it identified the social, political, economic, and technological forces shaping the issues of critical concern to people in the college's service area. Focusing on the specific issue they have been assembled to resolve, members of the coalition are able to identify and clarify for themselves the major forces shaping that issue from the perspective of the target public and the stakeholders. As part of their analysis, they should identify current programs and activities that address aspects of the issue. Most of these efforts will be represented by coalition members.

Identifying *who is affected by the issue* is probably the most important component of the issue statement. In mapping the target public and stakeholders, the community college's community-based programming management team should have answered this question to the best of its ability. As the coalition begins to form, however, the coalition must address the question again. While the target public is the primary focus of this effort, additional stakeholders may be identified as well. The coalition itself must ask the question, "Is everyone who needs to be here present at the table?" As study and analysis progresses, this question must be asked repeatedly, and the answer will affect both the statement of the issue and the membership of the coalition.

As the coalition members identify and analyze the factors surrounding the issue, they must also begin to identify *subissues.* Developing plans for addressing these subissues will be more manageable than trying to address the entire issue at once. To determine these subissues, the coalition must come to understand the target public's specific needs and any concerns that the target public and stakeholders have in relation to the issue. As the coalition lists and organizes factors affecting the issue, needs, and concerns, these subissues will begin to emerge. (See the examples of subissues that are presented in chapter 5.) These subissues must be deduced from the macro issue. This deductive connection is needed to maintain the collaborative effort for which the coalition has been striving, so the efforts will achieve the goals being envisioned for resolution of the issue.

Consider the nutrition and exercise issue used as an example earlier in the chapter. Through careful study and analysis of the issue and the forces affecting the well-being of the target public, the coalition in that example came to agreement on a refined definition of the issue. In collaboration with stakeholders and other resource persons, the coalition identified needs of the target public in relation to nutrition and exercise. Subject-matter specialists knowledgeable about health, nutrition, and exercise could also help the coalition members understand the needs and agree to group them into five subissues deduced from the broader issue. The subissues were (1) a reduction in fat intake; (2) a reduction in salt consumption; (3) a reduction in total caloric intake; (4) an increase in consumption of fruits, vegetables, and grains; and (5) an increase in the amount of exercise received. While nutrition and exercise experts help the coalition deduce these subissues from the macro issue, the leaders of the target public must also be involved because they know the target public's current habits and preferences and will share ownership in the changes that must occur.

Problem-Solving Techniques

The coalition will need to obtain a variety of information from diverse sources to study and analyze the issue, refine its definition, and come to agreement on the goals and strategies for its resolution. Certain collaborative problem-solving techniques for acquiring information, generating ideas, and reaching group decisions will be needed. The college's community-based programming management team can assist the coalition with facilitation techniques, such as those presented in the following paragraphs. More detailed descriptions of these techniques can be found in publications on group dynamics (see, for example, Garber, 1993).

Brainstorming or Brain Writing. *Brainstorming* can be used to generate as many ideas as possible about an issue without stopping to critique them. The purpose is to elicit everyone's thoughts, so the coalition can take all members' perspectives into consideration and develop strategies collaboratively. For example, coalition members might use brainstorming to generate a list of all the barriers to issue resolution of which they are aware.

Force Field Analysis. Coalition members can use *force field analysis* to identify and gain a clearer understanding of the forces that tend to help move the issue toward resolution and those that work against its resolution. The coalition can then look for methods to strengthen the forces promoting resolution and to weaken or eliminate the forces opposing it.

Affinity Diagrams. When a great number of ideas have been generated by the coalition, an *affinity diagram* can be constructed to help organize these ideas in a manner useful to the analysis (such as developing subissues). The result is a manageable number of categories instead of an unmanageable number of separate ideas.

Relations Diagrams. A perceived order in a problem or issue can sometimes be elucidated by means of a *relations diagram.* This type of diagram can help in developing an understanding of the forces affecting the issue and identifying the root causes of an issue by showing how these forces are related.

Nominal Group Technique. The *nominal group technique* is a structured process for generating ideas among coalition members and coming to a group selection of one or more of these ideas.

Developing a Vision

The community-based programming management team can help the coalition develop a vision to guide its work. The vision is manifest in the goal to be attained and will be useful to the coalition in deciding what strategies to use in resolving the issue. Coalition members cannot decide on useful strategies for resolving an issue if they do not know where they are trying to go. Building a vision involves developing *a description of what the situation in the target population will be if the issue is resolved.* These scenarios are "images" of how the situation will be altered as a result of the coalition's efforts to resolve the issue and set the goals for the plan of action. For example, the goal for the nutrition and exercise issue example discussed previously is for all citizens below the poverty level to have improved health. The vision or goal would be represented in a description of this healthy status—for example, body weights and cholesterol levels being within recommended standards, fewer major illnesses being reported, consumer habits being changed, and development of exercise facilities and programs being increased. Joel Barker (1991), in a videotape entitled "The Power of Vision," identified four elements of a "vision community" that suggest the type of vision needed for community-based programming. According to Barker, the vision community must be

■ leader initiated;

■ shared and supported;

■ comprehensive and detailed; and

■ positive and inspiring.

In community-based programming, the community college brings together the leaders of the target public and stakeholders who can create a vision that will be shared and supported by the community because they are legitimate spokespersons of the people they represent. The vision shared is like two-way communication: it comes from the people and returns to them in a continuing cycle of interaction. The study and analysis of the issue and the refinement of its definition by the leaders of the target public and stakeholders provide the basis for a comprehensive and detailed plan of action. Through collaboration and the guidance of the community-based programming management team, the coalition will develop a vision that is positive and inspiring. It is this shared vision produced through community-based programming that provides the driving force for resolving an issue and achieves what individuals and organizations acting alone are not able to accomplish.

For members of the community-based programming management team to assist the coalition in developing a collaborative plan of action (described in chapter 5), they must first help the coalition to study and analyze the issue, to refine the definition of that issue, and to decide upon the strategies that will be used to resolve it, as described in this chapter. This process will establish the base for further development of the coalition's vision for resolution of the issue, which will be embodied in the coalition's plan of action. Processual tasks 7 through 12 (processual tasks 11 and 12 are described in chapter 5) must be performed by the coalition in a manner that continues to maintain a collaborative atmosphere among coalition members. Without maintaining this spirit of collaboration, commitment to the coalition will falter because members will not see themselves and the people and organizations they represent as being empowered by the process. Community-based programming demands that the target public and stakeholders, as represented by their leaders, become empowered and assume responsibility for resolving an issue.

References

Barker, J. (1991). *The power of vision.* (Videotape). Burnsville, MN: Charthouse International Learning Corporation.

Bell, W., Hill, R., & Wright, C. (1961). *Public leadership.* San Francisco: Chandler Publishing.

Boone, E. (1985). *Developing programs in adult education.* Englewood Cliffs, NJ: Prentice-Hall.

Boone, E. (1992). Community-based programming: An opportunity and imperative for the community college. Raleigh, NC: North Carolina State University.

Boone, E., Dolan, R., & Shearon, R. (1971). *Programming in the Cooperative Extension Service: A conceptual schema.* Misc. Extension Publ. #72. Raleigh, NC: North Carolina Agricultural Extension Service.

Canfield, M. (1992). *Conflict resolution.* Fairfax, VA: Center for Policy Negotiation, George Mason University.

Feldman. D., & Arnold, H. (1983). *Managing individual and group behavior in organizations.* New York: McGraw-Hill.

Fisher, R., & Ury, W. (1981). *Getting to yes.* Boston: Houghton-Mifflin.

Garber, S. (1993). *A key to effective organizations: Small group problem-solving principles.* Raleigh, NC: North Carolina Cooperative Extension Service, North Carolina State University.

Gray, B. (1989). *Collaborating: Finding common ground for multiparty problems.* San Francisco: Jossey-Bass.

Katzenbach, J., & Smith, D. (1993). *The wisdom of teams: Creating high-performance organizations.* Boston: Harvard Business School Press.

Kuhn, A. (1982). *The logic of organizations.* San Francisco: Jossey-Bass.

Loomis, C. (1960). *Social systems: Essays on their persistence and change.* Princeton, NJ: D. Van Nostrand.

Melaville, A., & Bland, I. (1993). *Together we can.* Washington, DC: U.S. Department of Education, Office of Educational Research and Improvement.

Mulford, C. (1984). *Interorganizational relations: Implications for community development.* New York: Human Sciences Press.

Scholtes, P. (1988). *The team handbook.* Madison, WI: Joiner.

Tuchman, B., & Jensen, M. (1977). Stages of small group development revisited. *Groups and Organizations* Studies, 2, 419–27.

Developing and Implementing the Plan of Action

5

This chapter addresses the basic concepts, strategies, and skills for designing and implementing plans of action to resolve issues. It focuses on translating the decisions made by the coalition formed to address a specific issue (as described in chapter 4) into a functional plan that, if effectively implemented, will lead to resolution of the issue. Specifically, the chapter describes what is involved in implementing processual tasks 11 and 12.

Processual Task 11. The community college provides leadership for the coalition in translating its decisions into a unified plan of action.

Processual Task 12. The community college aids the coalition in implementing the plan of action by providing consultation, technical assistance, and opportunities for coalition leaders and other community leaders to report on progress made, discuss obstacles encountered, and explore the use of alternative strategies not included in the initial plan of action.

The implementation of these processual tasks is critical to the coalition's efforts in resolving the issue that has been selected as the focus of the college's community-based programming effort. Initiation of the design and implementation phase of the community-based programming process rests on several assumptions about the successful completion of the first 10 processual tasks.

1. The community college has institutionalized community-based programming. The president has established a community-based programming management team that functions as a part of his or her office and that has the responsibility of facilitating the college's involvement in community-based programming (processual tasks 1, 2, and 3).

2. The community college has established an environmental scanning committee, and that committee has conducted a thorough scan of the college's service area. Critical issues confronting people in the college's service area have been identified and ranked in priority order. The college's governing body has evaluated the ranked issues and given approval for the college to begin work on an issue (processual tasks 4, 5, and 6).

3. The issue that will become the focus of the college's initial efforts in community-based programming has been selected (processual tasks 5 and 6).

4. The community college's community-based programming management team, with the counsel and assistance of informed community leaders, has studied, analyzed, and mapped the target public who is directly affected by the issue and who must undergo change if the issue is to be resolved. Concurrently, the stakeholders who have a vested interest in the issue have been identified and studied (processual task 7).

5. The formal and informal leaders of the target public affected by the issue have been identified, and the chief spokespersons of the stakeholders have been identified (processual task 8).

6. The community college's community-based programming management team, with the assistance of informed community leaders, has engaged in dialogue with the leaders of the target public and stakeholders and has succeeded in getting these leaders to recognize the issue as important and as one that needs to be resolved. Further, those leaders have committed to working toward the resolution of the issue, and they have agreed upon the goal to be achieved (processual task 9).

7. A coalition of leaders from the target public and stakeholders has been formed and has analyzed the issue. The coalition has reached consensus on the issue to be resolved and what must be done to resolve it. The coalition, with the assistance of the community college's community-based programming management team, has (1) refined their definition of the issue; (2) formulated the goal to be pursued; (3) ana-

lyzed the macro issue to determine the subissues that are encompassed within that issue and that must be dealt with sequentially to resolve the larger issue; and (4) developed plans for resolving each subissue (processual task 10).

The actions embodied in these seven assumptions set the stage for the coalition, with the assistance of the community-based programming management team, to design the plan of action.

Designing the Plan of Action

The plan of action describes the steps that the coalition will take to resolve the defined issue. The plan, then, is a blueprint toward which the coalition directs its efforts in resolving the issue. The plan of action reflects the decisions reached by the coalition in implementing processual tasks 9 and 10. These decisions are translated into components that collectively constitute the plan of action. These components follow:

1. a statement of the macro issue;
2. clear articulation of the goal to be sought in resolving the issue;
3. a description of the target public for the macro issue;
4. a listing of the subissues encompassed in the macro issue; and
5. detailed plans for addressing and resolving each subissue encompassed in the macro issue, including the following elements:
   – a description of each subissue;
   – identification of the specific target public for each subissue. Note that the target public identified for the subissue will be a component or subset of the broader target public identified for the macro issue. (The target public for a macro issue generally includes a number of subgroups that are relevant to resolution of the issue.);
   – a formulation of one or more learner objectives for each subissue;
   – a description of the learning experiences and learner activities in which members of the target public will need to participate in order to acquire the behavior specified in each learner objective;
   – a schedule for implementing the learning activities for each objective;
   – identification of the resources required for implementing each learner activity;

Description of Macro Issue: _____

Goal(s) for Macro Issue: _____

Subissues Encompassed in Macro Issue: _____

Target Public: _____

Subissues	Target Public	Learner Objectives	Learner Activities & Change Strategies	Implementation Schedule	Resources	Responsibility	Expected Outcomes
# 1.							
# 2.							
# 3.							

Figure 4. Format for a plan of action.

- designation of responsibility—that is, a list of coalition members and other individuals who will provide the resources needed to resolve the issue and who will be responsible for implementing each learner activity; and
- a description of the outcomes expected for each objective.

Definition of Planning Terms

The components of the plan of action are defined as follows:

Macro Issue: A matter of wide public concern that is affecting or has the potential to affect the quality of life of a sizable group of people, referred to collectively as the *target public.*

Goal: A vision, or description, of the ideal state of affairs that would exist within the target public if the issue were resolved. The goal becomes the focal point toward which the plan of action and its implementation are directed.

Subissues: Smaller, manageable issues that are encompassed within and contribute to the macro issue and that must be dealt with through an ordered approach to resolve the macro issue.

Target Public: Those persons who will need to undergo change if the macro issue and its subissues are to be resolved.

Learner Objective: A description of the behavioral change that will need to occur in the target public for each of the subissues if the macro issue is to be resolved.

Learner Activities: The learning experiences in which the target public will need to participate to acquire the behavioral change specified in each learner objective.

Implementation Schedule (Timetable): The expected dates on which each learner activity will be conducted.

Resources: Educators and other people, facilities, printed materials, publicity, funds, and other resources required to implement learner activities.

Responsibility: The determination of and agreement on which members of the coalition or other people will be responsible for providing the resources for implementing each learner activity.

Expected Outcomes: The changes that are sought in the target public for each objective. Comparison of the actual outcomes to the desired outcomes indicates the extent to which each objective has been successfully achieved.

Figure 4 illustrates how these components can be presented in tabular form to make the order and relationships of the elements clear.

The *description of the macro issue* concisely identifies and describes briefly the major factors surrounding the issue, the people affected, and the subissues that are encompassed within the macro issue.

The *goal* statement specifies what the coalition expects to accomplish. It describes the ideal state of affairs that will characterize the target public upon resolution of the issue. The goal becomes the beacon toward which the attention and efforts of the coalition are directed in their quest to resolve the issue.

The *target public* statement identifies the people who will have to undergo change if the macro issue is to be resolved. In most cases, the target public encompasses a number of subgroups, each of which is relevant to resolution of one or more of the subissues.

Each of the *subissues* encompassed within the macro issue and derived from a deductive analysis of that broader issue is succinctly stated. The subissues are arranged in the order in which they are to be addressed by the coalition.

As shown in Figure 4, a detailed plan for resolving each subissue is developed. It begins with a definition of that component of the *target public* that must undergo change for the subissue to be resolved. For each subissue and its target public, *learner objectives* are formulated and clearly stated. These objectives describe the actions that members of the target public must take and behavioral changes that will need to occur if the subissue is to be resolved. The learner objectives provide the rationale for selecting and defining the *learning experiences* and *learner activities* in which the target public will need to participate to realize the specified behavioral changes. In selecting and describing learner activities, two questions should be addressed: (1) What learning activities will lead to the attainment of the objective? and (2) How can the activities be designed to facilitate learning?

An *implementation schedule* for the learning activities must be developed, agreed upon by the coalition, and included in the plan for resolving the subissue. Of particular importance, the *resources* that will be needed to implement each learner activity should be identified and listed. Resources may include, though are not limited to, educators and other resource people, facilities, time, funds, curriculum materials, and instructional aids. As shown in Figure 4, the coalition members and other individuals who will be responsible for providing the resources needed to implement each learner activity must be identified. For each objective, the coalition needs to define the *outcomes expected. Outcomes* are projections of results that are expected to be realized through the effective implementation of learner activities.

Plans of Action: Two Examples

Plans of action for two contemporary issues are illustrated in examples 1 and 2 presented at the end of this chapter. The broad issue addressed by example 1 is related to nutrition and exercise. The plan in example 2 was developed to resolve a water quality issue. These plans of action are illustrative of the content needed in effective plans.

As can be observed in both examples, the two macro issues (nutrition and water quality) encompass several subissues. Of particular note is the sequencing of the subissues. The premise is that an effective response to each of the macro issues will require a methodical approach, with each of the subissues being addressed and resolved through a carefully designed subsidiary plan of action. The outcomes in resolving each subissue are expected to contribute to the resolution of the macro issue and, ultimately, the attainment of the goal or goals that have been set by the coalition.

Implementing the Plan of Action

Once the plan of action has been designed, the coalition has the responsibility for its implementation (processual task 12). Although developing the plan of action is an essential component of the community-based programming process, implementing it is also critical to resolving the issue. The community college—through its community-based programming management team, which assumes the roles of leader and catalyst—is responsible for guiding and facilitating the efforts of the coalition in implementing the plans for resolving each of the subissues addressed in the plan of action.

As suggested earlier in this chapter and book, the objective of community-based programming is that the people, their leaders, and the stakeholders affected by an issue will become intensively involved in decisions about the issue and will collectively assume primary responsibility for its resolution. Thus, these leaders and stakeholders, functioning as a coalition, become the major action group in addressing and resolving the issue. The role of the community college and its community-based programming management team is to provide leadership for the coalition and to facilitate its team-focused effort to fully implement the plan.

The need to clarify and distinguish between the roles of the coalition and the community college at this stage in the community-based programming process is of paramount importance, for there is a danger that the distinction between the roles may become muddied. Of particular concern should be a mistaken perception among coalition members that the college is the dominant force in implementing the plan of action. This perception would seriously undermine the effectiveness of the coalition. Unless the coalition is indeed permitted and encouraged to assume responsibility for implementing the plan, its success in resolving the issue will be greatly diminished, as will be the commitment of community members to resolving the issue.

Critical questions about the expected roles of the coalition and community college in implementing the plan of action include the following:

1. What are the specific leadership actions that the community college will need to perform to enable the coalition to become organized?
2. How will the coalition prepare to follow through on implementing the plan of action?
3. What actions must the coalition take to implement the plan of action?
4. What actions will the community college need to perform as a catalyst and facilitator to provide the coalition the technical assistance and other forms of staff support it will need throughout the implementation process?

Let us examine questions one and two. The community college assumes the lead role in helping the coalition launch and implement its plan of action. Even though the coalition has been actively involved in developing the plan, it will need considerable help in becoming organized and prepared to follow through on implementation. In most cases, the newly formed coalition will have had little or no experience in functioning as a team. Through its community-based programming management team, the community college will need to help the coalition fully comprehend what is involved in implementing the plan. Attention should be focused on helping the coalition understand the resources, time, and effort to which its members must commit to implement the plan.

The community college's management team will also need to help the coalition develop an organizational plan and operating strategies that will guide the coalition's efforts throughout the implementation process. Particular emphasis should be given to helping the coalition consider how it will function as an organization. Decisions concerning the need for a chair, secretary, and steering committee must be made. The frequency, purposes, and agendas of meetings and other operational details will need to be determined. The coalition should be helped to explore strategies it can use to collect, process, and use feedback from individual coalition members and other individuals as they implement their assigned responsibilities. Further, the coalition will need assistance from the college's management team in developing a plan for reporting to the target public, stakeholders, and the community on the progress being achieved.

Beginning with its initial efforts to implement the plan of action and throughout the implementation process, *the coalition will need to keep its attention focused on the macro issue and the vision (goal) of the state of affairs that will exist if the issue is resolved.* Unless the issue and the plan for its resolution are continuously revisited throughout the implementation process, an inherent danger is that the coalition will become so engrossed with specific activities that it may lose sight of the issue and the role that the plan of action plays in resolving the issue.

The coalition must maintain a clear perspective on the subissues and how they are related to the macro issue. The identification of subissues encompassed in the macro issue and the specific plans for their resolution provide an effective road map for the coalition in its systematic quest to resolve the macro issue. The subissues are all interrelated and are an integral part of the macro issue. The orderly resolution of each of the subissues is critical to resolving the larger issue; thus, the coalition must continually be reminded that its actions in resolving a subissue are but a part of the larger plan for resolving the macro issue.

Throughout the implementation process, the coalition must function as a team. While individual members of the coalition will be assigned responsibilities for implementing specific learner activities, those individual efforts must always be viewed as a part of the overall plan of action. To maintain a team focus, the coalition will need to meet frequently, so members can interact, receiving and processing feedback on the status of the individual members' efforts. These meetings will lend assurance that what the coalition has planned is being implemented and is contributing to the team plan for resolving the subissue and the macro issue. Of particular importance is for the coalition to employ every means available to assure that the members are functioning as a team and that the efforts of each member are focused on resolution of the issue.

The coalition must continuously monitor and assess the results being achieved in implementing each learner activity. Through carefully planned formative evaluations of every decision made and action taken in implementing the plan of action, substantive feedback is obtained that should be used by the coalition in rethinking and altering those learner activities that are not producing the results envisioned. Systematically monitoring events and collecting feedback about the results being achieved can help the coalition keep its sights focused on the outcomes sought—namely, the resolution of the subissues and ultimately the macro issue. The lessons learned by the coalition members may strongly support the need for alterations in the plan of action. Learning which methods are working to produce the intended outcomes and which are not can keep the coalition on track as it moves toward resolution of the issue.

To maintain steady, positive movement toward resolution of the issue and its subissues, the coalition and its members must demonstrate accountability to the target public and stakeholders at all stages of the implementation process. Through planned meetings of the coalition, members who have been assigned responsibilities for providing resources and implementing learner activities should share the results of their efforts with the other coalition members. This action is needed in order to keep the coalition informed of progress; to provide feedback that can be used in revising elements of the plan, if necessary; and to assure that those who have agreed to accept responsibilities follow through in discharging those responsibilities. The coalition will also need to keep the target public, stakeholders, and other community leaders informed about its work and the results being achieved throughout the implementation process.

The fourth question addresses the actions that the community college will need to take in its role as a catalyst and facilitator as the coalition implements the plan. In general, the community college provides technical assistance and other forms of staff support. To implement this important role, the community college will need to engage in the following specific actions.

1. *Through the use of effective interpersonal and group process skills, the community college should guide the efforts of the coalition in implementing the plan of action.* Particular emphasis will need to be given to helping coalition members understand each of the subissues and how the resolution of those subissues contributes to the resolution of the macro issue. Further, the community college should continuously remind the coalition that it has the primary responsibility for implementing the plan of action and that the role of the college is to support the coalition in its efforts.

2. *The community college will need to help the coalition members become adept in the use of group process skills to facilitate the coalition's functioning as a team.* Effective implementation of the plan of action will require that the coalition members work as a team to bring to bear their combined resources and talents in resolving the issue. The community college should provide the coalition members with opportunities to learn group process skills and show them how to use those skills in helping the coalition to function as a team.

3. *Since individual members of the coalition, as members of a team, will be expected to assume the primary responsibility for implementing learner activities, the community college will need to help them understand and become skilled in the teaching-learning process.* The members, in most cases, will have had limited experience in planning for and effecting planned change in learner systems (that is, the target publics). Specifically, they will need to be helped to understand

    – how their assigned learning activity is an integral part of the larger plan;

    – how to understand and analyze both the culture and social organization of the target public as a basis for tailoring the learner activity to the situational context of the target public;

- how to define the behavioral changes that are expected to occur in members of the target public as a result of their participation in the planned learner activities;
- how to motivate members of the target public to participate actively in the learner activities;
- how to plan and implement learner activities;
- how to monitor learner activities to ensure that the intended change in the target public is occurring as well as how to process and use the feedback obtained to make needed changes in the learner activities;
- how to assess and measure the outcomes achieved in the target public through their participation in the learner activities; and
- how to report the results obtained and the lessons learned in implementing the learner activities back to the coalition so the coalition can strengthen its overall efforts to resolve the issue.

4. *Depending on the nature and complexity of the issue, the coalition may need help from the college in identifying and obtaining external technical expertise and resources.* Because of its connectivity within the community and throughout the nation, the community college can be instrumental in helping the coalition obtain the needed technical assistance.

5. *The community college should provide the coalition with the technical assistance that it will need to design and conduct ongoing formative evaluations of all the decisions made and actions taken with implementing all aspects of the plan of action.* Through planned evaluations and systematic monitoring, the coalition can gain valuable feedback and insights that will greatly facilitate efforts to implement the plan of action and to move toward resolving the issue. As the coalition implements activities called for in the plan of action, continuing formative evaluations, monitoring, and reporting will be areas that require particular and consistent attention.

The community college may need to help the coalition interpret and summarize the results of its efforts. Opportunities should be provided for frequent and continuing interaction among coalition members to enable them to connect learner activities and the results obtained to the plan of action and resolution of the issue. The following chapter discusses in greater detail the processes of assessing impacts and accounting for results to the target public and stakeholders.

Examples 1 and 2 are presented on the following pages.

Example 1. Nutrition Plan of Action

Macro Issue: A significant number of people in Tangipahoa Parish are experiencing health problems related to their nutrition and exercise practices. Information obtained by physicians and other health-care professionals indicates that nearly all of these people have limited resources and that their daily diets are too high in fat and too low in beta carotene. The major health problems include high cholesterol, high blood pressure, diabetes, and cancer.

Goal of Macro Issue: People who are experiencing nutrition-related health problems will change their diets to favor foods that are low in fat, low in salt, and high in complex carbohydrates and will engage in physical exercise, leading to improved health.

Subissues	Target Public	Objectives	Learner Activities	Implementation Schedule
1. Members of the target public consume diets too high in fat.	Adults 18 and over whose incomes are below the poverty line.	1A. Members of the target public will become aware of health risks associated with the consumption of high-fat-content foods.	Target public members will read about, discuss, and reflect on health risks associated with the consumption of foods high in fat content in neighborhood meetings. Local, state, and national rates of mortality and morbidity from chronic diseases related to diet and life-style will be discussed.	Easy-to-read printed materials will be designed, developed, and distributed to the target public in neighborhood meetings within a 6- to 8-week period.

Subissues Encompassed in Macro Issue: The macro issue includes five subissues, namely, (1) excessive fat intake, (2) excessive salt consumption, (3) excessive consumption of total calories, (4) inadequate consumption of fruits, vegetables, and grains (complex carbohydrates), and (5) inadequate exercise among members of the target public.

Target Public: Adults who are 18 or more years old and whose incomes are below the poverty line.

Resources	Responsibility	Outcomes
Activities, displays, and printed materials that address health risks associated with the consumption of fat and that are adapted to the target public's culture, language, and reading level.	County extension home economists, public health personnel, home economics teachers, and physicians. The target public's leaders will be involved in developing, adapting, and testing materials and activities.	Members of the target public will demonstrate an awareness of health risks associated with the consumption of high-fat-foods through focused group discussions.
Meeting places in the neighborhoods where the target public resides. Nutrition educators and leaders from the target public.	Neighborhood leaders, community center directors, YMCA outreach directors, school principals, and the clergy. County extension home economists, local home economics teachers, public health personnel, and other informed persons.	

continued

Subissues	Target Public	Objectives	Learner Activities	Implementation Schedule
		1A *(continued)*	Target public members will participate in neighborhood diagnostic screening to determine their cholesterol levels and their LDL/HDL ratio.	At least two initial screening sessions will be completed within two months in each of the neighborhoods in which members of the target public reside.
		1B. Target public members will know the foods that are high in fat content.	Target public members will learn about foods that are high in fat content and the health risks associated with their consumption in neighborhood meetings in which these foods are identified and discussed. Target public members will learn to read food labels, emphasizing fat and cholesterol content.	At least two meetings will be held within a two-month period in each of the neighborhoods in which members of the target public reside.

Resources	Responsibility	Outcomes
Facilities to conduct neighborhood diagnostic screenings	Neighborhood leaders and other informed persons to arrange for neighborhood sites to conduct screening tests.	Members of the target public will know their cholesterol levels and their LDL/HDL ratios.
Qualified health personnel to conduct screening process	Physicians, nurses, lab technicians, and other qualified persons	Members of the target public will know their risk of cardiovascular disease as it relates to their cholesterol levels and their LDL/HDL ratios.
Proper medical supplies and equipment to conduct neighborhood screenings	Public health officials, physicians, nurses, and other qualified persons	
Publicity for neighborhood screening sessions	Neighborhood leaders, newspaper and radio editors, clergy, school personnel, and people representing other channels of communication	
Easy-to-read printed materials about high-fat foods and risks associated with their consumption that are adapted to the target public's culture, language, and reading level	County extension home economists, local home economics teachers, public health personnel, members of the medical profession, and other informed persons. The leaders of the target public will be involved in developing, adapting, and testing printed materials and activities.	In focused group discussions, target public members will demonstrate knowledge of foods that are high in fat content and the health risks associated with their consumption.
Food product nutrition labels		
Meeting places in the target public' s neighborhood	YMCA outreach director, school principals, directors of community centers, and neighborhood leaders	
Publicity for meetings	County extension home economists, public health information personnel, directors of community centers, local radio stations, clergy, and neighborhood leaders	
Nutrition educators and discussion leaders	County extension home economists, local home economics teachers, public health personnel, members of the medical profession, and other informed persons	

continued

Subissues	Target Public	Objectives	Learner Activities	Implementation Schedule
		1C. Target public members will change daily intake of foods to include less animal fat and reduce daily total grams of fat consumed	Target public members will discuss the Food Guide Pyramid and how to follow it while eating a diet lower in fat. Target public members will plan menus to include foods low in fat content. Target public members will participate in neighborhood meetings in which the selection and preparation of low-fat foods are demonstrated and discussed. Taste tests will be held. Target public members will discuss barriers to choosing lower-fat foods and meals and how to overcome these barriers.	Meetings to teach menu planning and the preparation of low-fat foods will be held in each neighborhood within two months after the diagnostic screening of the target public.

Resources	Responsibility	Outcomes
Meeting places and facilities in local neighborhoods conducive to teaching how to plan menus and prepare low-fat foods	Community center directors, YMCA outreach directors, school principals, and neighborhood leaders	In neighborhood meetings, target public members will identify low-fat foods and demonstrate how to incorporate them into their menus.
Publicity for neighborhood meetings	Neighborhood leaders, clergy, county extension home economists, and other persons	Target public members will demonstrate appropriate serving sizes and number of servings from food groups.
Nutrition educators and discussion leaders Food Guide Pyramid chart Food models, measuring cups, plates, sample foods Restaurant menus, recipes	County extension home economists, local home economics teachers, public health personnel, and other informed persons in the target public	In neighborhood meetings, target public members will demonstrate how to prepare low-fat foods as a part of their menus.

continued

Subissues	Target Public	Objectives	Learner Activities	Implementation Schedule
2. Members of the target public consume diets too high in sodium	Adults 18 and over whose incomes are below the poverty line	2A. Target public members will become aware of the health risks associated with the overconsumption of salt and know the foods that are high in salt content.	In neighborhood meetings, target public members will read about, discuss, and reflect on health risks related to the overconsumption of salt.	Easy-to-read printed materials will be designed, developed, and distributed to the target public in neighborhood meetings within a 6- to 8-week period.
			Target public members will discuss family tree as it relates to hypertension and stroke.	
			Target public members will measure out sodium content of favorite high-sodium foods for comparison with sodium guidelines	
			Target public members will read about, discuss, and reflect on the sources of the sodium in their diets.	

Resources	Responsibility	Outcomes
Printed materials on foods high in salt and the risks associated with their consumption that are adapted to the target public's culture, language, and reading level	County extension home economists, local home economics teachers, public health personnel, and physicians. Leaders of the target public will be involved in developing, adapting, and testing printed materials.	In focused group discussions, target public members will demonstrate awareness of health risks associated with the consumption of foods high in salt content.
Meeting places in the neighborhoods where the target public resides	Community center directors, YMCA outreach directors, school principals, and neighborhood leaders	In focused group discussions, target public members will demonstrate knowledge of foods high in salt content.
Publicity for neighborhood meetings	Public health information personnel, neighborhood leaders, clergy, radio stations, newspapers, and other channels of communication	
Nutrition educators and discussion leaders	County extension home economists, local home economics teachers, public health personnel, members of the medical profession, and other informed persons	
Displays showing salt content of selected foods and amounts equivalent to sodium guidelines		

continued

Subissues	Target Public	Objectives	Learner Activities	Implementation Schedule
		2A *(continued)*	Target public members will participate in neighborhood diagnostic screening to determine their blood pressure levels.	At least two blood pressure screening sessions will be held within a two-month period in each neighborhood where members of the target public reside.

Resources	Responsibility	Outcomes
Neighborhood facilities at which to conduct on-site diagnostic screenings	Neighborhood leaders and other informed persons to arrange for neighborhood sites to conduct screening tests	Members of the target public will know their blood pressure levels.
Qualified health personnel to administer screening tests.	Medical doctors, nurses, laboratory technicians, and other qualified health practitioners	
Proper medical supplies and equipment to conduct neighborhood screenings	Medical doctors, nurse practitioners, and laboratory technicians	
Publicity for neighborhood screening sessions	Neighborhood leaders, radio, newspapers, clergy, school personnel, and other channels of communication	

continued

Subissues	Target Public	Objectives	Learner Activities	Implementation Schedule
		2B. Target public members will change their daily intake of foods to include less salt.	Target public members will discuss the Food Guide Pyramid and how to follow it while moderating their salt intake. Target public members will plan menus that include foods low in salt. Target public members will read food labels, especially for the sodium content. Target public members will participate in neighborhood meetings in which the preparation of low-salt meals is demonstrated and discussed. Target public members will discuss barriers to reducing salt consumption and how to overcome those barriers.	Two meetings in which menu planning is taught and the preparation of foods low in salt is demonstrated will be held in each neighborhood within two months following the diagnostic screening.

Resources	Responsibility	Outcomes
Neighborhood meeting places	Neighborhood leaders, school principals, and community center directors	In neighborhood meetings, target public members will be able to identify low-salt foods and demonstrate how to incorporate them into planned menus
Publicity for neighborhood meetings	Neighborhood leaders, clergy, radio stations, newspapers, and other influential informants	
Nutrition educators and discussion leaders	County extension home economists, home economics teachers, public health nutritionists, and other informed resource persons	In neighborhood meetings, target public members will demonstrate how to prepare low-salt food.
Product food and nutrition labels		

continued

Subissues	Target Public	Objectives	Learner Activities	Implementation Schedule ➡
3. Members of the target public consume a diet too high in calories.	Adults 18 and over whose incomes are below the poverty line	3A. Target public members will know the health risks associated with consuming a diet too high in calories.	In neighborhood meetings, target public members will read about, discuss, and reflect on health risks associated with the excessive consumption of calories.	Easy-to-read printed materials about high-calorie foods and the health risks associated with their consumption will be developed and distributed within a two-month period.

At least two meetings in which foods high in calorie content are discussed will be held within a two-month period in each neighborhood in which the target public resides. |

Resources	Responsibility	Outcomes
Printed materials on the excessive consumption of calories that are adapted to the target public's culture, language, and reading level	County extension home economists, home economics teachers, public health nutritionists, and medical personnel. Leaders of the target public will be involved in developing or adapting printed materials.	In focused group discussions, target public members will demonstrate awareness of health risks associated with the excessive consumption of foods high in calories.
Neighborhood meeting places	Community center directors, YMCA outreach directors, school principals, and neighborhood leaders	In focused group discussions, target public members will demonstrate knowledge of health risks associated with the consumption of foods high in calorie content.
Appropriate means of distributing materials	Health department public relations staff, local newspapers, schools, clergy, and neighborhood leaders	
Publicity for neighborhood meetings	Health department public relations officers, community center directors, local radio stations, newspapers, clergy, and neighborhood leaders	
Nutrition educators and discussion leaders	County extension home economists, home economics teachers, public health nutritionists, and other informed resource persons	

continued

Subissues	Target Public	Objectives	Learner Activities	Implementation Schedule
		3B. Target public members will change their daily intake of foods to consume fewer calories if they have been overconsuming.	Target public members will participate in neighborhood diagnostic screenings to determine their weight, height, and waist-to-hip ratio. Target public members will plan menus that include low-calorie foods.	At least two initial screening sessions will be completed in each neighborhood within a six-week period.
			Target public members will participate in neighborhood meetings in which the preparation of low-calorie meals Is demonstrated and discussed.	Within six weeks of diagnostic screening of target public participants, neighborhood meetings will be held in which menu planning is taught and the preparation of foods low in calories is demonstrated.

Resources	Responsibility	Outcomes
Facilities to conduct on-site diagnostic screening	Medical doctors, nurses, public health personnel, and leaders of the target public	Target public members will know their suggested total calorie consumption range or level.
Qualified health personnel to administer the screening process	Physicians, nurses, and public health personnel	In neighborhood meetings, target public members will be able to identify low-calorie foods and demonstrate how to incorporate them into planned menus.
Proper medical supplies and equipment to conduct on-site screenings	Physicians, nurses, and public health personnel	
Publicity for neighborhood screening sessions	Neighborhood leaders, radio stations, newspapers, clergy, school personnel, and other community sources	In neighborhood meetings, target public members will demonstrate how to prepare foods low in calorie content.
Meeting places in neighborhoods	Community center directors, YMCA outreach directors, school principals, and neighborhood leaders	
Publicity for neighborhood meetings	Radio stations, newspapers, clergy, and neighborhood leaders	
Nutrition educators and discussion leaders	County extension home economists, home economics teachers, and public health personnel	

continued

Subissues	Target Public	Objectives	Learner Activities	Implementation Schedule
4. Members of the target public need to increase their consumption of fruits, vegetables and grains (complex carbohydrates)	Adults 18 and over whose incomes are below the poverty line	4A. Target public members will know the health benefits associated with the consumption of high-complex-carbohydrate diets and foods that are high in complex carbohydrates, such as fruits, vegetables, and grains.	In local neighborhood meetings, target public members will read about, discuss, and reflect on health benefits related to fruit, vegetable, and grain consumption.

Target public members will discuss barriers to consumption of fruits, vegetables, and grains and how to overcome those barriers. | Easy-to-read materials on the benefits of the consumption of fruits, vegetables, and grains will be developed and distributed to the target public within a 6- to 8-week period.

At least two meetings in which the benefits of consuming fruits, vegetables, and grains (complex carbohydrate diets) are discussed will be held within a two-month period in each neighborhood in which members of the target public reside. |

Resources	Responsibility	Outcomes
Printed materials that embody the target public's culture, language, and reading level	County extension home economists, school home economists, physicians, and public health personnel. Leaders of the target public will assist in developing, adapting, and testing printed materials.	In focused group discussions, target public members will demonstrate awareness of health benefits associated with fruit, vegetable, and grain consumption.
Appropriate means of distributing materials	Public health information officers, radio stations, clergy, and neighborhood leaders of the target public	In focused group discussions, target public members will demonstrate knowledge of health benefits associated with fruit, vegetable, and grain consumption.
Publicity for neighborhood meetings	Health department public relations personnel, directors of community centers, radio stations, newspapers, clergy, and neighborhood leaders	
Meeting places in neighborhoods	Community center directors, YMCA outreach directors, school principals, and neighborhood leaders	
Nutrition educators and discussion leaders	County extension home economists, home economics teachers, and other informed persons	
Fruit, vegetable, and grain displays		

continued

Subissues	Target Public	Objectives	Learner Activities	Implementation Schedule ➡
		4B. Target public members will change their daily intake of foods to include more fruits, vegetables, and grains (complex carbohydrates).	Target public members will plan menus that include fruits, vegetables, and grains.	Within two months neighborhood meetings will be held in which menu planning is taught and the preparation of meals high in fruits, vegetables, and grains (complex carbohydrates) is demonstrated.
			Target public members will participate in neighborhood meetings in which the preparation of meals high in fruits, vegetables, and grains (complex carbohydrates) is demonstrated and discussed.	

Resources	Responsibility	Outcomes
Neighborhood meeting places and facilities for teaching menu planning and demonstrating the preparation of foods	Neighborhood leaders, clergy, school personnel, and other channels of communication	Target public members will know their suggested total calorie consumption range or level.
Publicity for neighborhood meetings	Community center directors and YMCA outreach directors	Target public members will be able to identify fruits, vegetables, and grains as complex carbohydrate foods and demonstrate how to incorporate them into planned menus.
Nutrition educators and discussion leaders	County extension home economists, home economics teachers, public health nutritionists, and other informed resource persons	
Fruit, vegetable, and grain displays.		Target public members will demonstrate knowledge of how to prepare fruits, vegetables, and grains.

continued

Subissues	Target Public	Objectives	Learner Activities	Implementation Schedule
5. Members of the target public do not get enough exercise.	Adults 18 and over whose incomes are below the poverty line	5A. Target public members will become aware of the health benefits associated with exercise.	Target public members will read about, discuss, and reflect on health benefits associated with regular exercise. Target public members will discuss barriers to regular exercise and how to overcome those barriers.	Easy-to-read printed materials will be designed, developed, and distributed to the target public in neighborhood meetings within a 6- to 8-week period.
		5B. Target public members will exercise appropriately and regularly or will know how and why to do so.	Target public members will learn about various exercises and how to determine appropriate exercises and levels of exercise for themselves. Target public members will participate in planning their own exercise program.	At least two meetings will be held within a two-month period in each of the neighborhoods in which members of the target public reside.

Resources	Responsibility	Outcomes
Activities and printed materials that address health benefits associated with regular exercise and that are adapted to the target public's culture, language, and reading level	County extension home economists, school home economists, physicians, and public health personnel. Leaders of the target public will assist in developing, adapting, and testing printed materials.	Through focused group discussions, target public members will demonstrate an awareness of health benefits associated with exercise.
Meeting places in the neighborhoods where the target public resides	Public health information officers, radio stations, clergy, and neighborhood leaders of the target public	
Nutrition educators, exercise physiologists, and discussion leaders; key leaders from the target public	Community center directors, YMCA outreach leaders, school principals, physical education teachers, exercise physiologists, and neighborhood leaders	
Easy-to-read printed materials and videotapes about exercises and how to do them safely that are adapted to the target public's culture, language, and reading level	County extension home economists, school home economists, physicians, and public health personnel. Leaders of the target public will assist in developing, adapting, and testing printed materials and videotapes.	Target public members will demonstrate (or have knowledge of) appropriate and regular exercise.
Meeting places and exercise areas in the target public's neighborhoods	Neighborhood leaders of the target public	
Publicity for meetings	Health department public relations personnel, directors of community centers, radio stations, newspapers, clergy, and neighborhood leaders	
Nutrition educators, exercise physiologists, and discussion leaders	Community center directors, YMCA outreach leaders, school principals, physical education teachers, exercise physiologists, and neighborhood leaders	
Key leaders from the target population		

Example 2. Water Quality Plan of Action

Macro Issue: Recent representative tests indicate that Smith County's water supply is becoming increasingly contaminated for several reasons. The county's agriculture is undergoing a rapid transition from traditional row-crop production to highly intensified hog and poultry production and processing. Further, the county is experiencing an influx of small manufacturing firms. Accompanying these changes is an increase in the construction of new houses for persons moving into the county to fill the jobs created by the new industries. Evidence suggests that the new agricultural industries and manufacturing firms are inadvertently releasing substances into the environment that are contaminating the county's water supply. A check on selected houses that have been constructed within the last 10 years reveals that some of their septic tanks are beginning to malfunction prematurely. Of major importance are (1) the seeming lack of knowledge possessed by county residents and county officials about the water problem and its potential consequences on human and other forms of life, (2) the lack of county ordinances to control and manage wastewater from agricultural and manufacturing industries that release pollutants into the environment, and (3) the lack of building standards regulating the construction and maintenance of residential septic tanks.

Goal of Macro Issue: Eliminate or reduce to a safe level the discharge into the environment of pollutants and contaminants that are hazardous to a safe, sustainable supply of potable water for human consumption and other uses.

Subissues Encompassed in Macro Issue: The macro issue includes a number of subissues, namely, (1) county residents and other stakeholders (i.e., county officials, public service agencies, and regulatory groups) lack knowledge about contaminants that are being released into the county's water supply; (2) county residents, county officials, public service agency personnel, and regulatory officials are not knowledgeable about the true risks associated with contaminants being released into the water supply; (3) industry leaders are not fully knowledgeable about sources of chemicals and other contaminants detected in water supplies; (4) county residents and significant stakeholders lack knowledge about "the basinwide concept" and how contaminants outside the county find their way into the county's water supply; (5) industry leaders (i.e., manufacturing firms and agricultural enterprises) are not fully knowledgeable about the effects of toxic substances being released from their operations into the county's water supply nor are they skilled in leading dialogue about the potential risks and effects on the water supply; (6) the building industry is not knowledgeable about standards and regulations that must be followed in siting, sizing, and constructing residential septic tanks; (7) county officials, public health personnel, and regulatory agency officials have not developed standards and regulations nor the means of enforcing them to ensure that manufacturing and agricultural industries develop and implement measures for controlling the release of toxic substances into the county's environment and water supply; and (8) existing laws are not adequate to require industries and homeowners to control release or *report* the release of pollutants into the environment and water supply.

Target Public: Residents of Smith County, elected county and state officials, public service agencies, regulatory groups, industry leaders, public interest groups, and other significant stakeholders.

Subissues	Target Public	Objectives	Learner Activities	Implementation Schedule
1. Members of target public lack knowledge about contaminants being released into the county water supplies and the sources of those contaminants.	County residents County officials Public service agency personnel Regulatory agency personnel	1A. Members of the target public will become knowledgeable about contaminants being released into the county water supplies.	Members of the target public will read about, discuss, and reflect on contaminants being released into the county water supplies and their effects on human and other forms of life.	Easy-to read printed materials will be developed and distributed to the target public within a three-month period.
		1B. Members of the target public will be able to identify potential sources of nutrients, oxygen-demanding materials, and potentially toxic substances.	Members of the target public will obtain and discuss records from regulatory agencies.	Public hearings on the issue will be held in communities within a three-month period.

Resources	Responsibility	Outcomes
Printed materials that address contaminants and their effects on the water supply	Public health agencies, environmental groups, Cooperative Extension Service	Members of the target public will demonstrate knowledge of water contaminants.
Public-interest news releases that address the issue	Public health agencies, environmental groups, Cooperative Extension Service	
Meeting places for public hearings	Community leaders and school officials	
Self-monitoring reports	Regulatory agencies and other sources	

continued

Subissues	Target Public	Objectives	Learner Activities	Implementation Schedule
		1C. Members of the target public will be able to list known sources of contaminants that are being released into the county's water supply and to identify suspected sources.	Members of the target public will read about, investigate, and discuss the various sources of water contaminants.	Published results of tests on the operations of the agricultural industry, manufacturing firms, and malfunctioning septic tanks will be provided to the target public within a three-month period.
2. Members of the target public are not knowledgeable about the true risks associated with contaminants being released into the county water supplies.	County residents County officials Public service agency personnel Regulatory agency officials	2A. Members of the target public will become more knowledgeable about the true risks associated with contaminants being released into the water supplies.	Members of the target public will contact purveyors of water and toxicologists who can describe scientifically valid health and environmental risks associated with each water contaminant.	Public meetings will be scheduled within three months after implementation of a testing program to explain results of tests and describe risks associated with each contaminant.

Resources	Responsibility	Outcomes
Findings of tests conducted on the operations of industrial and agricultural sources	Environmental agencies, public health agencies, and other groups	Members of the target public will know the sources of water contamination.
Scientific test results and trusted toxicologists: EPA Water Hotline (1-800-624-8301)	Community groups, state agencies, and county health departments	Members of the target public will gain knowledge about risks of water contaminants.

continued

Subissues	Target Public	Objectives	Learner Activities	Implementation Schedule
3. Industry leaders are not fully knowledgeable about sources of chemicals and other contaminants detected in water supplies.	Industry leaders (i.e., manufacturers and agricultural producers and processors)	3A. Industry leaders will be able to identify specific industrial processes that are sources of chemicals and other contaminants detected in water supplies.	Industry leaders will identify and discuss specific industrial processes that are sources of chemicals and other contaminants in water supplies.	Industry leaders will assess and discuss unit processes as soon as contaminants are detected.
4. County residents and other stakeholders lack knowledge about "the basinwide concept" and how contaminants outside the county find their way into county water supplies.	Residents of the entire river basin and legislators empowered with crafting legislation aimed at protecting environmental quality and water supplies	4A. Members of the target public will become more knowledgeable of how waste and other water quality insults along the entire basin affect local water quality. Members of the target public will be able to list out-of-county sources of contaminants found in county water supplies.	Members of the target public will obtain monitoring reports of river quality and, through a series of information meetings, begin deciding which sources of contaminants will be addressed.	River-basin-wide informational meetings will be conducted over a three-month period. Actions to be taken will be formulated within three months of final implementation. Additional educational meetings will be scheduled to present an action plan to citizens six months after the initial educational meetings.

Resources	Responsibility	Outcomes
Water test results; material safety data sheets and reports	Industry groups, personnel managers, health and safety personnel	Industry leaders will develop production methods that use fewer potentially dangerous chemicals and that use such chemicals in lower volumes.
Meeting places along the basin Summaries of regulatory agency monitoring data Information on interrelations of water quality trends along the basin.	Cooperative Extension Service and state water quality regulatory agency, local government agencies, and councils of government	Members of the target public will demonstrate knowledge of various pollution sources, water quality issues, and threats to health and environmental and water quality from various sources within the entire river basin. Agencies will develop interlocal groups to mitigate pollution sources.

continued

Subissues	Target Public	Objectives	Learner Activities	Implementation Schedule
5. Industry leaders are not fully knowledgeable about the effects of toxic substances being released from their operations into county water supplies nor are they skilled in leading dialogue about potential risks and effects of those substances on county water supplies.	Industry leaders (i.e., agricultural producers and processors and manufacturing firms)	5A. Members of the target public will become fully knowledgeable about the toxic substances being released from their operations into county water supplies and will commit to taking the appropriate measures to control their releases.	Members of the target public will read about and discuss the effects of the release of toxic substances into the environment and water supply.	Printed materials, published test results, and other information pieces will be prepared and disseminated to industry leaders within a three-month period.
		5B. Industry group leaders will become more skillful in communicating risks to the affected target public.	Members of the target publics will discuss the measures that they must take to control the release of toxic substances being produced by their operations into the environment and water supplies.	Meetings of industry leaders and others will be held within a three-month period to discuss measures that they will need to take to manage their operations so as to prevent the release of toxic substances into county water supplies.

Resources	Responsibility	Outcomes
Printed materials, test results, and other information pieces	Public health agencies, environmental agencies, and regulatory groups	Members of the target public will know and commit to the appropriate measures to control and manage their operations to eliminate or reduce to a safe level the release of toxic substances into county water supplies.
Meeting places and informed discussion leaders	County officials, the Cooperative Extension Service, environmental agencies, and public health agencies	

continued

Subissues	Target Public	Objectives	Learner Activities	Implementation Schedule
6. The home-building industry is not knowledgeable about standards and regulations that must be followed in siting, sizing, and constructing residential septic tanks.	Home building industry leaders Bankers and leaders of the mortgage industry	6A. Members of the target public will know and commit to the standards that must be followed in constructing septic tanks.	Members of the target public will meet to discuss the standards that must be followed in constructing septic tanks.	Printed materials will be distributed to homebuilders within a six-month period.
		6B. Target public will understand the consequences of loan default and lawsuit potential with poor septic systems.	Members of the target public will list and discuss consequences of improper siting, sizing, installation, and operation of systems.	Meeting of target public will be held within a 6- to 12-month period.

Resources	Responsibility	Outcomes
Printed materials that define the standards for constructing and maintaining residential septic tanks	Public health personnel, county officials, and environmental agencies	Members of the target public will know and follow appropriate standards in constructing residential septic tanks.
Meeting places	Public health agencies, county officials, and industry leaders	Members of the target public will assure that loans are available only when assurance of system integrity has been provided.

continued

Subissues	Target Public	Objectives	Learner Activities	Implementation Schedule
7. County public health personnel and regulatory agency officials have not developed adequate standards and regulations nor the means of enforcing them to ensure that industries develop and implement measures for controlling the release of toxic substances into county water supplies.	County regulatory agency and public health personnel	7A. Members of the target public will develop effective regulations on the release of toxic substances into the county water supplies and the means for ensuring industry compliance.	Members of the target public will confer with state and federal experts and other waste management experts to learn about local ordinances needed to control the operations of industry to prevent the release of toxic substances. Members of the target public will draft ordinances and choose the means for their effective enforcement.	Meetings will be held with state and federal officials and other waste management experts within a three-month period. Work sessions will be held within a three-month period to enable county officials and others to develop ordinances and means for ensuring compliance.

Resources	Responsibility	Outcomes
Meeting places Printed materials	Cooperative Extension Service, public health agencies, county officials, and industry leaders	Members of the target public will develop regulations for controlling the waste management operations of industries.
Meeting places Printed materials that provide insight into regulations and regulatory practices being followed in other counties	County officials EPA personnel, health officials	Members of the target public will develop the appropriate means for enforcing regulations.

continued

Subissues	Target Public	Objectives	Learner Activities	Implementation Schedule
8. Existing laws are not adequate to ensure that industries and homeowners control or report the release of pollutants into water supplies.	Elected officials	8A. Elected officials will pass laws to facilitate development of rules that control release and require reporting of the release of toxic substances and other pollutants into the county water supplies.	Elected officials will discuss local requirements with regulatory agencies and stakeholders and will draft legislation conducive to reporting and control. County regulatory agencies will adopt a record-keeping program for industries to report releases of contaminants.	Discussion groups will convene during the upcoming legislative season, and participants will become strong advocates for the passage of adequate legislation. County agencies will contact industries and discuss reporting.

Resources	Responsibility	Outcomes
Meeting places, informed printed materials, videotapes, discussion leaders and conveners	University faculty members, Cooperative Extension Service personnel, state agency personnel, legislators, industry personnel, and stakeholder groups	Elected officials will pass legislation protecting water supplies.
Industry self-reports	County health officials, Cooperative Extension Service personnel, chamber of commerce members	County will have reports on file with public agencies.

Evaluation and Accountability

6

All of the decisions made in the community-based programming process—beginning with the institutionalization of community-based programming and extending through the measurement and reporting of outcomes—should be subjected to an ongoing process of evaluation. This chapter focuses on evaluation and accountability in community-based programming and presents approaches for implementing processual tasks 13, 14, and 15.

> **Processual Task 13.** *The community college provides leadership for the coalition in assessing the outcomes achieved toward resolving the issue and in determining the cost-effectiveness of the plan of action.*

> **Processual Task 14.** *The community college arranges for and helps coalition leaders to report to their respective constituencies, agencies, organizations, and other stakeholders on the progress made toward resolving the issue.*

> **Processual Task 15.** *The coalition uses the results of the plan of action and lessons learned through its implementation to develop and implement new strategies for continued efforts toward resolving the issue.*

Since the issue being addressed is likely to be complex, the coalition's first attempt to resolve it is not likely to be completely successful.

Therefore, the coalition's efforts usually will be progressive and evolutionary. After each successive attempt at resolving the issue, improvements will be made in the plan of action to produce better results with the next planning and implementation cycle. The information gained through the evaluation conducted during each cycle is important in measuring the success of the plan of action, reporting outcomes to stakeholders, and using lessons learned to improve the plan of action.

The *issue* is the driving force in community-based programming. It provides the basis for identifying the target public and stakeholders—those who are affected by the issue. Once the target public and stakeholders have been clearly delineated, the next critical task is to identify and interact with the leaders of the target public and spokespersons for the stakeholders. The intent is to form a coalition of these leaders, so they can reach consensus on the issue and develop a plan of action (blueprint) for resolving it.

Evaluation is a critical part of community-based programming because it brings the process full circle. Determining which strategies have been successful in carrying out processual tasks 11 and 12 (see chapter 5) provides a basis for making decisions about needed improvements in the plan of action. It also provides information needed to report to stakeholders and others on the effectiveness of the coalition's efforts to resolve the issue.

The evaluation, like the development of the plan of action, must be sharply focused on resolving the defined issue. The major underlying assumption for this chapter is that processual tasks 1 through 12 have been implemented effectively. Successful completion of processual tasks 13, 14, and 15 is expected to produce specific outcomes. The evaluation process determines whether these outcomes have been achieved. If the coalition's first plan of action has not fully resolved the issue, the evaluation can provide key information that can be useful in planning and implementing a second effort to resolve the issue. The expected outcomes for processual tasks 13, 14, and 15 follows:

- an objective and valid assessment of summative outcomes attained through implementation of the coalition's plan of action;
- the dissemination of information about the coalition's outcomes to those holding the coalition accountable; and
- use of lessons learned through evaluation of the coalition's efforts in planning and implementing subsequent attempts to resolve the issue.

Continuous Evaluation in Community-Based Programming

Evaluation must be an integral part of every processual task in community-based programming. Formative evaluation is a planned, continuing process that focuses on the critical assessment of every decision and choice made in implementing each of the 15 processual tasks in the community-based programming process. The formative evaluation process begins when the community college decides to engage in community-based programming, and it encompasses the examination of all subsequent decisions, choices, and actions.

For each processual task, outcomes are specified. Through systematic, ongoing evaluation, the processes and activities pursued to achieve these outcomes are subjected to rigorous scrutiny and assessment to determine their effectiveness. Feedback obtained is used to revise and alter the processes and activities to assure the greatest possible impact in achieving the intended outcomes. Each action taken during the course of every processual task should be reviewed and evaluated to identify opportunities for increasing the college's effectiveness and efficiency in carrying out community-based programming. *Although evaluation is a component of each processual task, it takes on increasing importance in the development and implementation of the plan of action and the measurement of outcomes achieved (see chapter 5).*

Relationship of Evaluation to the Plan of Action

Summative evaluation in community-based programming is directed toward determining the extent to which the coalition has achieved the goals and objectives set forth in the plan of action and to determine the extent to which the issue has been resolved or has moved toward resolution. The community college, through its community-based programming management team (see chapters 1 and 3), should encourage and remind members of the coalition to develop a summative evaluation plan while developing their plan of action. The evaluation plan should outline how the coalition will evaluate learner objectives, learner activities, and resource utilization. Each learner objective set forth in the plan of action should specify at least one measurable outcome that can be assessed in the evaluation process.

It is important for community college leaders to remember that changes in the plan of action should be reflected in plans to evaluate outcomes. Whenever the plan of action is revised as a result of monitoring (formative evaluation), the evaluation plan should be adjusted accordingly. For example, if the coalition elects to abandon one of its objectives, that objective should also be deleted from the evaluation plan.

Summative Evaluation for Impact Assessment

Processual Task 13. The community college provides leadership for the coalition in assessing the outcomes achieved toward resolving the issue and in determining the cost-effectiveness of the plan of action.

Because evaluation is a key function of the coalition and because each member may bring a different perspective to the task, it is important for all coalition members to be actively involved in the evaluation process. As in other components of the community-based programming process, collaboration and consensus-building are essential tools in evaluation (see chapter 4). In planning the evaluation process, collaboration and consensus-building are vital because they maximize the utility of the evaluation findings to coalition members and others who hold the group accountable (Patton, 1982).

The primary objective of processual task 13, simply stated, is to provide evidence that changes related to the issue being addressed can be attributed to implementation of the coalition's plan of action. As part of its plan of action, the coalition should develop an evaluation plan for assessing the final outcomes of its efforts. Summative evaluations are "conducted *after* completion of the program...(or after stabilization) and for the benefit of some external audience" (Scriven, 1991, p. 340). The process of assessing final outcomes is known in the evaluation profession as *impact assessment*. The primary objective of processual task 13 is to conduct a summative impact evaluation.

To provide useful and accurate information, a summative impact evaluation must be tightly coupled with the coalition's plan of action and should represent collective agreement among coalition members about expected outcomes that are expressed in terms of effects upon the issue being addressed. A summative impact assessment plan should include the following elements:

- clear and concise articulation of the issue being addressed;
- clear and concise articulation of the coalition's goal, usually presented as a vision of what conditions would be like in the community college's service area if the issue were fully resolved;
- articulation of subissues and learner objectives along with the learner activities and resources devised to carry out each objective;
- expected outcomes for each objective;
- specific indicator(s) for each expected outcome to determine whether each objective has been achieved; and
- data collection and analysis processes.

A suggested format for the recording and presentation of these components of the evaluation plan is presented in figure 5. In the following paragraphs we will explore these components in greater detail.

Elements of a Summative Impact Assessment Plan

Clear and concise articulation of the issue being addressed. An example of a completed evaluation plan is presented as example 3. Because the issue drives the community-based programming process, formulating a clear, concise issue statement is essential to the success of the coalition in achieving expected outcomes.

In the example of a coalition formed to address the issue of health problems related to nutrition (see the example in chapter 5), the issue statement might be: "A significant number of people in Tangipahoa Parish are experiencing health problems related to their nutrition practices. Information obtained by physicians and other health-care professionals indicates that nearly all of these people have limited resources and that their daily diets are too high in fat, salt, and sugar and too low in beta carotene. The major

Description of Macro Issue: _____

Goal(s) for Macro Issue: _____

Subissues Encompassed in Macro Issue: _____

Target Public: _____

Subissues	Target Public	Learner Objective(s)	Learner Activities	Expected Outcomes	Indicator(s) of Outcomes	Data Sources

Figure 5. Format for a community-based programming evaluation plan.

Description of Macro Issue: A significant number of people in Tangipahoa Parish are experiencing health problems related to their nutrition practices. Information obtained by physicians and other health-care professionals indicates that nearly all of these people have limited resources and that their diets are too high in fat, salt, and sugar and too low in beta carotene. The major health problems include cardiovascular diseases, diabetes, and cancer.

Goal(s): People who are experiencing nutrition-related health problems will change their diets to include foods that are low in fat, low in salt, and high in complex carbohydrates, resulting in improved health.

Target Public: Adults who are 18 or more years old and whose incomes are below the poverty line.

Subissues	Target Public	Learner Objective(s)	Learner Activities	Expected Outcomes	Indicator(s) of Outcomes	Data Sources
1. Reduction in fat intake.	Adults 18 or more years old and below the poverty line.	Members of target public will become aware of the health risks associated with the consumption of foods high in fat content.	In neighborhood meetings, members of target public will read about, discuss, and reflect on health risks associated with the consumption of foods high in fat content.	Members of target public will demonstrate awareness of health risks associated with the consumption of foods high in fat content.	Articulation of health problems related to high-fat diets.	Pretest and posttest data on ability of target public members to identify health problems related to high fat consumption.

continued

Example 3. Community-Based Programming Evaluation Plan

Subissues	Target Public	Learner Objective(s)	Learner Activities	Expected Outcomes	Indicator(s) of Outcomes	Data Sources
2. Reduction in salt consumption.	Adults 18 or more years old and below the poverty line.	Members of target public will become aware of the health risks associated with the consumption of a high-salt diet.	In neighborhood meetings, members of target public will read about, discuss, and reflect on health risks associated with the consumption of excessive salt.	Members of target public will demonstrate awareness of health risks associated with high salt consumption.	Articulation of health problems related to high-salt diets.	Pretest and posttest data on ability of target public members to identify health problems related to high salt consumption.
3. Reduction in total calories consumed	Adults 18 or more years old and below the poverty line.	Members of target public will become aware of the health risks associated with consumption of a high-calorie diet.	In neighborhood meetings, members of target public will read about, discuss, and reflect on health risks associated with the consumption of excessive calories.	Members of target public will demonstrate awareness of health risks associated with consumption of high-calorie foods.	Articulation of health problems related to high-calorie diets.	Pretest and posttest data on ability of target public members to identify health problems related to high-calorie diets.

continued

Example 3. Community-Based Programming Evaluation Plan—*continued*

Subissues	Target Public	Learner Objective(s)	Learner Activities	Expected Outcomes	Indicator(s) of Outcomes	Data Sources
4. Increased consumption of fruits, vegetables, and grains (complex carbohydrates).	Adults 18 or more years old and below the poverty line.	Members of target public will become aware of the health benefits associated with the consumption of fruits, vegetables, and grains.	In neighborhood meetings, members of target public will read about, discuss, and reflect on health benefits associated with the consumption of fruits, vegetables, and grains.	Members of target public will demonstrate awareness of health benefits associated with fruit, vegetable, and grain consumption.	Articulation of health benefits related to consumption of fruits, vegetables, and grains.	Pretest and posttest data on ability of target public members to identify health benefits related to diets rich in fruits, vegetables, and grains.
5. Increase in exercise.	Adults 18 or more years old and below the poverty line.	Members of target public will become aware of the health benefits associated with increased exercise.	In neighborhood meetings, members of target public will read about, discuss, and reflect on health benefits associated with regular exercise.	Members of target public will demonstrate awareness of health benefits associated with exercise.	Articulation of health benefits related to regular exercise.	Pretest and posttest data on ability of target public members to identify health benefits related to regular exercise.

Example 3. Community-Based Programming Evaluation Plan—*continued*

health problems related to this issue include high cholesterol, high blood pressure, diabetes, and cancer." This statement specifies the macro issue (health problems related to nutrition practices) and identifies the health problems of most concern (high cholesterol, high blood pressure, diabetes, and cancer), so everyone clearly understands the specific issue and the subissues being addressed by the coalition. Clearly stating the issue helps to keep the summative impact assessment process focused.

Clear and concise articulation of the coalition's goals, usually presented as a vision of what conditions would be like in the service area if the issue were fully resolved. A common source of problems in summative impact evaluation is imprecision or ambiguity in the goal statement. A vague goal statement can indicate that the coalition is unsure of the outcomes expected from implementing a plan of action. Unless goal statements are clear and specific, identifying and measuring expected outcomes is virtually impossible. Goals should be both clear and measurable. If attainment of the goal cannot be measured, no matter how clearly the goal is stated, the coalition members will have difficulty drawing conclusions about their progress.

One good way to develop a goal statement is to phrase it as an ideal— that is, in language that reflects the coalition's vision for the community college's service area if the issue were to be fully resolved. An example of a goal statement phrased as an ideal would be the following: "People who are experiencing nutrition-related health problems will change their diets to include foods that are low in fat, low in salt, and high in complex carbohydrates, resulting in improved health." This goal is clear and measurable because it indicates when the issue can be considered to be resolved (when the target public eats a diet that is low in fat, low in salt, and high in complex carbohydrates). Once the goal is clear and has attained the general agreement of coalition members, the coalition can then turn its attention to the question, "How can we determine whether we have reached this goal?"

Articulation of subissues, learner objectives, and the learner activities, and resources needed to achieve each learner objective. The plan of action includes specific subissues that, when resolved, will lead to resolution of the macro issue. Learner objectives are developed for each subissue, and for each learner objective the plan specifies learner activities to be implemented. These learner activities should have a close, logical connection to the learner objective, which should also have a logical link to the plan of action's subissue. (For more information on learner activities in the plan of action, see chapter 5.)

It is important to consider the implementation process when conducting the summative impact evaluation. Detailed evaluation results can be very helpful when it comes time to reflect on lessons learned from implementing the plan of action. Suppose that the summative impact evaluation indicated that the coalition was not successful in resolving the issue. Further examination might indicate that a key learner activity either was not implemented at all or was implemented incorrectly. This finding would enable the coalition to correct the oversight by implementing the learner activity properly during the next attempt to resolve the issue.

Another reason for examining learner activities is to assess whether the activity can be reasonably expected to lead to reduction or resolution of the macro issue. Providing learner activities that are not linked to the subissue, even if those activities are perfectly implemented, will lead to failure. For example, imagine that the coalition's plan of action called for development of printed materials containing nutrition information but that the materials used terms unfamiliar to the target public. Even if the materials were used correctly, the efforts would be unsuccessful because the materials were not suitable for the target public. Including in the summative impact evaluation process a review of the learner activities, based on good monitoring data for each activity, can be useful in identifying reasons for attaining or failing to attain the outcomes sought.

Expected outcomes for each objective. An expected outcome is a result that the coalition expects to attain by implementing the plan of action. Each learner objective should specify at least one expected outcome. Otherwise, the coalition should reexamine its rationale for establishing the objective.

It is important to differentiate between a learner objective and an outcome. A *learner objective* is an action to be taken, and the *outcome* is the result of that action. For example, in addressing the health issue the coalition might identify a subissue of reducing fat intake. Connected to this subissue would be the learner objective of "making the target public aware of the health risks associated with the consumption of high-fat-content foods." (See the plan of action in chapter 5.) The outcome might be that "the target public will demonstrate an awareness of the health risks associated with the consumption of high-fat foods." The connection is that as a result of *making* the target public *aware* of the health risks associated with fat consumption, members of that public can *demonstrate* this awareness in focused discussions; that is, they can articulate the health risks associated with high-fat diets.

Expected outcomes can be either *manifest* or *latent.* Manifest outcomes are "evident, obvious, observable immediately" (Boone, 1985, p. 178). For example, if members of the target public reduce the fat consumed in their diets as they participate in the learner activities set forth in the coalition's plan of action, that would be a *manifest outcome. Latent outcomes,* on the other hand, often do not become evident until some time after the coalition's implementation of the plan of action has been completed (Boone, 1985). For example, members of the target public who participated in the coalition's learner activities might experience weight loss and lower cholesterol levels long after their participation in the coalition's learner activities was completed.

When establishing expected outcomes, the community-based programming management team should press the coalition members to indicate whether they expect quick results or results that could possibly take a long time to materialize. In considering the results of an evaluation, the community-based programming management team should facilitate the coalition's discussion on whether an expected outcome did not materialize or whether the outcome is latent and will become evident in the distant future. This distinction will help the coalition determine whether a learner activity was ineffective or whether it had simply not been implemented over a long enough period to draw conclusions about its success.

In addition to helping assess expected outcomes, the community-based programming management team should help the coalition be alert to unexpected outcomes. Programs often have effects that were not anticipated but merit being mentioned to those who hold the group accountable. Looking only for anticipated effects can lead to missed opportunities for discovering and reporting successes. For example, imagine that, by changing their eating and exercise behavior, members of the target public increased the proportion of muscle and decreased the amount of fat in their body's composition, and their bones became stronger. Those outcomes would be worth reporting to anyone interested in the coalition's work. Identifying unexpected outcomes could also lead to the discovery of ill effects that outweigh the successes gained in addressing the issue. Possible unexpected outcomes should be anticipated and documented as the plan of action is being implemented, so the effects of those outcomes can be considered when making decisions about refining the coalition's planned learner activities.

Specific indicator(s) for each expected outcome. An *indicator* is documented evidence that supports the coalition's claims regarding the outcomes of collaborative actions taken to address an issue. Indicators lend credibility to the conclusions drawn about the success of the coalition's efforts and provide a basis for making recommendations for future actions. An indicator is a measure of the expected outcome. For example, the number of participants regularly attending learner activities would be an indicator of the success or failure of efforts to recruit participants among the target public. A sign-in sheet at each learning session could document that outcome. Documented evidence can be either *quantitative* (a numerical measure, such as a percentage change in the condition) or *qualitative* (a descriptive measure, such as a chronology of the condition).

Documented evidence should be both *valid* and *reliable*. A *valid* measure "reflects the concept it is intended to measure" (Rossi & Freeman, 1993, p. 232). Morris, Fitz-Gibbon, & Lindheim (1987) suggest that the validity of a measure should be assessed by determining whether it is an appropriate measure of what the coalition wants to know. For example, checking the temperatures of those participating in the coalition's learner activities would not be a valid measure of the knowledge gained by the target public regarding the health risks associated with the consumption of fat: body temperature does not measure knowledge.

Determining the validity of indicators is essential and requires clear, logical thought. Suppose that a coalition evolved to address the issue of nutrition-related health problems and that it established a goal of reducing the incidence of nutrition-related health problems among low-income adults. Also suppose that the evaluation plan called for nutrition knowledge to be measured by the frequency of attendance at learner activities. This measure would be invalid because the concept being measured would be attendance, not nutrition knowledge. A more appropriate measure would be a test to determine the target public's knowledge of nutrition.

Assessing validity is not always as easy as in this example. Clarity in stating the learner objective can be of tremendous benefit. The learner objective should clearly indicate what is to be measured (for example, nutrition knowledge), and expected outcomes should be stated in measurable terms (for example, increased knowledge of nutrition, increased ability to identify high-fat foods, and increased frequency with which nutritionally sound foods are consumed).

A *reliable* measure is one that would produce the same results if the data collection process were repeated, assuming that the conditions remained unchanged (Rossi & Freeman, 1993). In assessing whether an indicator is reliable, the coalition should determine whether the indicator produces consistent data that are free of unpredictable errors (Morris, Fitz-Gibbon, & Lindheim, 1987). For example, a reliable measure of an adult's cholesterol would be a blood test because blood tests always report blood content.

Data collection and analysis processes. After indicators of outcomes have been established, careful thought should be given to collecting data. Ideally, data collection occurs during implementation of the plan of action. Data collection should be both systematic and accurate. The important guiding principles in data collection are (1) to collect only the data needed and (2) to avoid missing crucial data. Without careful thought, it is easy to collect data that are of little or no value to the evaluation process. Collecting data, no matter how interesting, that do not lend insights into the extent to which the specified issue has been resolved is an inefficient use of coalition resources. All data collected should help the coalition draw conclusions about the success of its work. Conceivably, the majority of the data needed for a summative impact evaluation might be collected during the monitoring process because many summative impact evaluations use data collected over time to detect changes in the issue being addressed (see chapter 5).

A problem often encountered in evaluation is missing data. Some data collection opportunities occur only once, and being unprepared to collect the data when available could leave gaps in knowledge regarding the success or failure of the coalition's efforts. The monitoring process (see chapter 5) can be helpful in identifying critical data that are not being collected if evaluation is indeed an integral part of the coalition's work.

In addition to identifying the specific data needed, the coalition should consider the credibility of the data, which depends in part on the source. Credible data sources are those that report data that is as accurate, valid, and reliable as possible in the real world. Official data (such as state or federal reports or reports from private research organizations) can usually be considered credible.

Primary source data are preferable to *secondary source data. Primary source data,* simply stated, are data collected by direct observation or measurement. For example, if our health coalition wanted to determine whether the eating behavior of participants was improving, observing the content of participants' meals would provide primary source data. Perceptions about the participants' dietary practices by the persons implementing the learner activities would be *secondary source data.* Usually, primary data sources are the target publics when the intent is to collect data on improvements in the target public's performance.

The data collected in a summative impact evaluation are analyzed to determine whether the coalition's efforts achieved the expected outcomes set forth in the plan of action. In assessing the net effect of a coalition's efforts, data reflecting the issue's *magnitude* (number of people affected) and *scope* (area affected) both before and after implementation of the coalition's efforts are essential. This approach is known as a *pretest-posttest evaluation design.* In this design, data are collected before the plan of action is implemented (the *pretest*), the "treatment" (implementation of the plan of action) then occurs, and data are again collected after implementation has been completed (the *posttest*). For example, imagine that the coalition addressing nutrition-related health problems needed to determine whether the target public's awareness of foods with high-salt content increased. The coalition might ask participants (the target public) to respond to a predetermined set of questions regarding their knowledge of salt content in foods. Participants would then engage in learner activities, after which they would again be asked to respond to the same set of questions. The net difference in the number of items answered correctly would reflect the extent to which the learner activities were effective. Data on the magnitude of the issue obtained before implementing the plan of action are called *"benchmark"* data and are obtained as a part of the issue analysis process (see chapter 3).

Data on the magnitude of the issue after implementation of the plan of action should be obtained through a systematic and *planned* (regularly scheduled) data collection process both during and immediately after implementation of the plan of action. The data obtained will provide the coalition members with insight into trends or patterns (for example, whether they are moving toward or away from success). The difference between the pre-implementation and post-implementation data form the basis for drawing conclusions about the effectiveness of the coalition's efforts. Data collected between pre- and post-implementation assessments help to put the conclusions from the summative impact evaluation into proper context. (See the section "Profiting from Lessons Learned by Capitalizing on Strengths and Avoiding Pitfalls" later in this chapter.)

The coalition should carefully reflect on the relationship between implementing the learner activities in the plan of action and the cost of implementing those activities (for example, costs for staff, facilities, and supplies). Given the effort that is likely to be needed in procuring resources, the efficient use of those resources is vital to the ultimate resolution of the issue and to the continued support of coalition members.

Guiding Questions for Summative Evaluation

The following questions are provided as a guide to help the community-based programming management team facilitate the coalition's efforts in developing and implementing a summative impact evaluation plan. The questions are intended to guide the team in thinking about possible obstacles to the coalition's work in processual task 13. Although these questions are not all-inclusive, they provide a good foundation and framework for the community college's management team to enable the coalition members to begin the summative impact evaluation process.

Goal Assessment

■ What issue is the coalition addressing? Is there consensus on the issue? Is there a division among coalition members regarding the issue? If there is a division, is it potentially detrimental to the ultimate success of the coalition's efforts to resolve the issue?

■ How many people are distressed by the issue? How are people affected? What is the trend of the issue's severity (for example, increasing,
increasing rapidly, or decreasing)? What geographic area is most
affected by the issue?

■ What is the coalition trying to accomplish? What is the ultimate
"vision" regarding the issue; that is, what conditions would exist if the
issue were fully resolved? Is there consensus among coalition members regarding this vision?

■ What specific results are expected? What are the primary goals of this
effort to resolve the issue? Are there secondary goals? Which goals
are most important to the coalition?

■ What plan (program) is being implemented to address the issue? Does
the plan of action include reasonable means to address the issue at
hand? Does the plan of action address the issue or a symptom of the
issue? Does it matter which is being addressed?

Goal Attainment

■ What objectives were accomplished as a result of implementing the
coalition's plan of action? Can these results be attributed to something
other than the coalition's efforts?

■ What objectives were partially accomplished? How can success be
enhanced? Are the alternatives for enhancing success feasible?

■ What objectives were not attained? Is there a discernible reason? Is it
reasonable to expect the objectives to be attained if the program is
modified?

■ What unintended outcomes occurred while implementing the plan
of action? What latent outcomes are likely to occur in the distant
future?

Cost-Benefit Analysis

■ Did coalition members contribute resources as expected? If not,
did the lack of resources affect the success of the program? If so,
how?

■ How much did the coalition spend collectively in implementing the
plan of action? Was this more or less than the expected cost of
implementation?

■ Can the benefits (results) of the plan of action be quantified? Why or why not? If benefits can be measured, do they justify the program expenditures?

Accountability in Community-Based Programming

> **Processual Task 14.** *The community college arranges for and helps coalition leaders to report to their respective constituencies, agencies, organizations, and other stakeholders on the progress made toward resolving the issue.*

Because in addressing the issue several organizations will have contributed resources, it is important to let stakeholders and the target public know whether the collaborative efforts of the coalition have been productive. In addition, reporting results can be an effective means for keeping coalition members informed about and committed to resolving the issue. If results are positive, reporting them can help gain the support of stakeholders who may have initially resisted becoming involved. Reporting the coalition's success can also help recruit other members of the target public to participate in the coalition's further efforts to resolve the issue.

The community college should lead the coalition in specific work during the implementation of processual task 14, primarily

■ reporting outcomes to the target public and its leaders;

■ reporting outcomes to the leaders of stakeholder groups and their constituencies; and

■ reporting outcomes to community college leaders, governance officials, faculty members, and members of the environmental scanning committee.

Reporting Outcomes to the Target Public and Their Leaders

Evaluation outcomes should be reported to members of the target public in terms they can easily understand, as opposed to using the technical jargon of stakeholders and other professionals. For example, it would be appropriate to inform adults experiencing nutrition-related health problems about the success of a nutrition program in layman's terms. The most effective and efficient medium for informing target publics of the coalition's efforts is through their formal and informal leaders. Having their leaders deliver the message gives the outcomes more credibility among members of the target public.

Reporting Outcomes to the Leaders of Stakeholder Groups and Their Constituencies

The means of delivering the message to stakeholders and their leaders is important, but with these groups the focus should be on identifying the audience(s) to be reached. Disseminating information on the effectiveness of the coalition's efforts provides an opportunity to identify other stakeholders who should be involved. In community-based programming, the intent is "to draw the circle large," and that concept should apply to disseminating results as well. Under ideal circumstances, the coalition includes leaders of organizations that contributed resources to the coalition's efforts. These leaders will need to report the coalition's results to their respective organizations. Again, choosing the best method for presenting evaluation results should be given careful consideration. Presenting outcomes in voluminous narratives using complicated tables and complex language reduces the utility of the evaluation. Concise, accurate information presented in an interesting format will have a better chance of being used and valued by stakeholders and their constituencies.

Reporting Outcomes to Community College Leaders, Governing Officials, Faculty Members, and Members of the Environmental Scanning Committee

Because the community college initiated the collaborative efforts to resolve the issue through community-based programming, people in all areas of the college should be informed of the progress made. Familiarity with the coalition and its outcomes helps those within the community college to speak knowledgeably of the coalition's actions, the college's involvement in those actions, and the results. Keeping members of the community college informed enhances internal support of community-based programming and can serve as a recruitment tool to increase participation of the faculty in future community-based programming efforts.

Guiding Questions for Accountability Through Reporting

The following questions are provided as a guide to help the community-based programming management team facilitate the coalition's efforts in its accountability and reporting obligation. The questions are intended to guide the team in thinking about possible obstacles to the coalition's work in processual task 14. Although these questions are not all-inclusive, they provide a good foundation and framework for the community college's management team to enable the coalition members to begin the accountability and reporting process.

Reporting Outcomes to Target Publics

- Who are the target public(s) for this issue? Who are their formal leaders? Who are their informal leaders?
- How can information best be presented?
- Who can best carry the message of the coalition's results?

Reporting Outcomes to Stakeholders

- Who are the stakeholders for this issue? Who are their formal leaders? Who are their informal leaders?
- Are there stakeholders who are not part of the coalition? If so, who are they? Should they be notified of the coalition's results?
- How can information best be presented?

Reporting Outcomes to the Community College Community and Environmental Scanning Committee

- Who can best carry the message?
- What is the best means of distributing this information?

Using Lessons Learned

Processual Task 15. *The coalition uses the results of the plan of action and lessons learned through its implementation to develop and implement new strategies for continued efforts toward resolving the issue.*

Because most issues are broad and complex, it is unlikely that the coalition will develop a perfect plan of action to resolve the issue completely on the first attempt. The need for the coalition's continued efforts to resolve the issue will usually be evident, and the coalition should launch a renewed effort when this need becomes clear. The lessons learned from the summative impact evaluation should be used as a resource in shaping the coalition's subsequent planning efforts. The cycle of reviewing the results, revising the plan of action, and implementing the revised plan should continue until the issue has been fully resolved.

Continuous assessment through monitoring activities, such as systematic data collection and analysis, provides support and direction for revisions in the plan of action. The summative evaluation conducted upon first implementation of the plan of action can be thought of as an interim summative evaluation that is repeated periodically until the issue is resolved. Through continuous, systematic data collection and analysis, the coalition can make adjustments before the program gets too far off course. The results of the evaluation process, along with the inputs from those who hold the coalition accountable, provide direction for coalition efforts to continue until the issue is completely resolved.

The community college should lead the coalition in specific activities during the implementation of processual task 15. These activities include:

■ determining whether to continue or discontinue coalition activities; and

■ profiting from lessons learned by capitalizing on strengths and avoiding pitfalls.

Determining Whether to Continue
or Discontinue Coalition Activities

Coalitions are intended to be temporary in the sense that they should exist only as long as the issue exists. Once the issue has been resolved, the coalition should dissolve. By reviewing data collected in the implementation process, the community-based programming management team should provide leadership for determining whether and how the plan of action should be modified in a new effort to address the issue or whether the time has come for the coalition to cease its activities. The management team should facilitate the coalition's efforts to review evaluation findings for decision-making purposes. The principal criterion in deciding whether the coalition should continue to function is whether the issue being addressed is still pressing and merits attention. If the issue continues to diminish the quality of life for large numbers of people in the college's service area, there is justification for the continued existence of the coalition. As the coalition revisits and revises its plan of action, it is conceivable that its membership might need to change. Some members might drop out of the coalition while new members might be added.

Profiting from Lessons Learned by Capitalizing
on Strengths and Avoiding Pitfalls

Boone (1985) observes that evaluation is the process that closes the loop on program development activities. Given the complexity of most issues and the scope of involvement in the coalition's development and implementation of its plan of action, it is a reasonable assumption that the initial plan will not be perfect and will need some revision in order to achieve optimum results. The community college, in its effort to be a leader and catalyst in community-based programming, should regularly remind the coalition of evaluation results and the implication of those results for refinements in the plan of action as it is developed and implemented.

The first task is to determine whether the coalition's plan of action resolved or caused positive movement toward resolution of a specific issue. After final outcomes have been assessed, the coalition should explore the question, "Why was the program successful or unsuccessful?" so findings can be translated into lessons learned. Those lessons can then guide the future course of action.

Determining why a program was successful or partially successful should focus on identifying the learner activities in the plan of action that should be retained, refined, or eliminated from future coalition efforts to resolve the issue. For example, if the coalition's summative impact evaluation indicated that the efforts had a positive effect on the adoption of sound nutrition habits by the target public, but upon closer analysis it is discovered that some learner activities were not good investments of coalition resources, the coalition would likely use these findings as a basis for deciding to continue the coalition's efforts but would modify the plan of action by abandoning learner activities that were not cost-effective. If, however, the coalition discovered, through the documented evidence of the summative impact evaluation, that some learner activities were very successful and relatively low in cost, then the coalition would likely decide to continue those learner activities.

Guiding Questions for the Coalition's Future Actions

The following questions are recommended as a guide to help the community-based programming management team facilitate the coalition's effort in planning a second and subsequent efforts to resolve the issue. The questions are intended to guide the management team in thinking about possible obstacles to the coalition's work in processual task 15. Although these questions are not all-inclusive, they provide a good foundation and framework for the community college's management team to enable the coalition members to begin the replanning process.

Determining Whether to Continue or Discontinue the Coalition

- What progress was achieved in the first coalition effort?
- Should coalition efforts regarding the issue continue or discontinue? Why?
- If efforts discontinue, is the issue likely to continue or recur?
- If efforts continue, should the composition of the coalition be modified in some way, such as by adding or deleting members?

Determining Whether the Current Plan of Action Should Be Modified and in What Way

■ Should coalition efforts be modified? If so, how?

■ How are changes in the plan of action likely to resolve the issue?

■ Is there an additional cost involved in the modifications? If so, are resources available?

Because community issues tend to be broad and complex, we have seen that they are not likely to be resolved in a coalition's first effort. Future efforts to address the issue remain the responsibility of the coalition. The impact assessment results and the lessons learned in implementing the initial plan of action are invaluable tools for making decisions regarding improvements in the second and subsequent cycles of planning and implementation. The community college, through its community-based programming management team, should facilitate the coalition's use of evaluation findings and lessons learned during each cycle of implementation by encouraging the meaningful involvement of all coalition members.

References

Boone, E. J. (1985). *Developing programs in adult education.* Englewood Cliffs, NJ: Prentice-Hall.

Morris, L. L., Fitz-Gibbon, C. T., & Lindheim, E. (1987). *How to measure performance and use tests.* Newbury Park, CA: Sage.

Patton, M. Q. (1982). *Practical evaluation.* Newbury Park, CA: Sage.

Rossi, P. H., & Freeman, H. E. (1993). *Evaluation: A systematic approach.* (5th ed.) Newbury Park, CA: Sage.

Scriven, M. (1991). *Evaluation thesaurus.* (4th ed.) Newbury Park, CA: Sage.

Community-Based Programming in Retrospect: Observations and Recommendations

7

The community-based programming process is deeply anchored in the premise that a healthy, viable community is characterized by an empowered people who are connected with its institutions. This connectedness is manifest in the spirit with which the people, public agencies, and community organizations collaborate to apply their combined resources and talents in confronting and resolving critical issues. This premise provides the foundation for ACCLAIM's community-based programming process. Described in the first six chapters of this book, the model provides a rational and systematic process for the involvement and sustained collaboration of people, their leaders, and their community's agencies and organizations in confronting and resolving those issues that are negatively affecting, or have the potential to affect adversely, the quality of life of the community and its people.

At the center of the community-based programming process and critical to its success are the nation's community colleges. Serving at times as leader and other times as catalyst, the community college is the one organization that has the resources, experience, impartiality, and desire to bring together various segments of its community to focus on broad-based community issues.

ACCLAIM, through its pilot demonstration colleges, has subjected its community-based programming model process to rigorous tests and validated its effectiveness. It has observed and documented the positive outcomes that can accrue to both the community college and its community through implementation of the community-based programming process. These outcomes include the following:

■ an elevated role for the community college in its service-area community, especially becoming recognized and accepted as a community leader by the people who reside in that service area and by significant community stakeholders, including county boards of commissioners, school boards, chambers of commerce, economic development commissions, and many other county agencies and organizations;

■ increased visibility and recognition of the significant role that the community college can play in helping people learn to work together in confronting and resolving issues;

■ increased resources from local sources, including financial support from business and industry;

■ increased cooperation among the people, public agencies, and community organizations in collectively seeking to improve the quality of life of the community and its people;

■ increased participation in the programs and activities of the college among those individuals and organizations that previously had little or no contact with the college;

■ greater involvement of people from all walks of life in decisions affecting their welfare and the governance of their communities;

■ greater recognition of and acceptance by the community college's staff of the importance and complexity of the community and the active role of the college in the affairs of the community; and

■ increased support for the community college by the people and local governing groups, as manifested by increased funding from elected officials and by the willingness of citizens to become advocates for the community college.

Observations and Recommendations

Through its work with the pilot demonstration community colleges in North Carolina, South Carolina, Virginia, and Maryland, ACCLAIM has had a fertile laboratory in which to study and learn about the practical aspects of implementing the community-based programming process. This rich experience has enabled the ACCLAIM faculty to observe and identify those factors that are critical to success. These observations, along with recommendations to community college leaders who have an interest in expanding their college's roles to incorporate community-based programming, are presented here.

Observation 1

Community colleges that achieve major strides in engaging in community-based programming are led by presidents who understand and are committed to the community-based programming process. These presidents are knowledgeable about what is required to implement community-based programming. Through their study of the process and an assessment of how their colleges can adapt and become involved in community-based programming, these presidents have become committed to leading their colleges in becoming community-based institutions.

Recommendation

Community college presidents who have an interest in increasing their college's involvement in the affairs of their service-area communities should learn about the community-based programming process and the benefits it can provide to their community colleges and to their service-area communities.

Observation 2

Community colleges that have experienced success in implementing the community-based programming process initially developed and adopted a definition of community-based programming that is congruent with their organizational culture and the dynamics of their respective communities. The definition is the product of collaboration among the college's administrators, faculty, support personnel, and members of its governing board.

Recommendation

The president of the community college should involve the college's administrators, faculty, support staff, and governing officials in developing, reaching consensus on, and adopting a definition of community-based programming that is compatible with the college's culture and that can be used in pursuing their professional responsibilities at the community college and in the community.

Observation 3

In those community colleges that have experienced the greatest success in community-based programming, leaders have acquired a substantial knowledge base about their service-area communities and the dynamics of the social, economic, political, and technological factors encompassed within those communities. Armed with that understanding, these community college leaders envisioned how community-based programming could play a significant role in enhancing the quality of life for residents and in optimizing the use of resources in the service-area communities.

Recommendation

Under the leadership of the community college president, the community college should engage in intensive study and analysis of its community to enhance its knowledge of the community and understand the role that community-based programming can have in improving the quality of life of the community's people.

Observation 4

Community colleges that have experienced the greatest success in implementing the community-based programming process have carefully and effectively incorporated community-based programming into their mission, philosophy, organizational structure, and goals. Further, these community colleges have adjusted the allocation and organization of their resources, as well as their modes of operation, to facilitate their involvement in community-based programming.

Recommendation

The community college president should involve the college's administration, faculty, support staff, and governing officials in reinterpreting and revising, where appropriate, their college's mission, philosophy, goals, organizational structure, and mode of operation to assimilate and accentuate the community-based programming process as an integral part of the college's operation.

Observation 5

Community colleges that have established community-based programming management teams to facilitate and guide the college's implementation of the community-based programming process have experienced greater success than those colleges that have assigned this responsibility to one staff member. Functioning as an integral part of the office of the college president, these management teams have become highly skilled in guiding their college's implementation of the community-based programming process.

Recommendation

The community college should establish, empower, and use a community-based programming management team to guide and facilitate its efforts in implementing the community-based programming process. This team should be a function of the president's office and, ideally, should be led by a high-level community college administrator.

Observation 6

The success of the community college in engaging in community-based programming is significantly associated with its staff's and governing board's understanding of the community-based programming process. Those ACCLAIM pilot demonstration colleges that have been successful in their community-based programming efforts have placed considerable emphasis on providing formal training for their staff, governing officials, and community leaders in the community-based programming process. Further, these successful community colleges have provided the funds needed for participation in that training.

Recommendation

Community colleges that engage in community-based programming should provide formal training for their staff, governing officials, and community leaders in community-based programming. Funding and released time must be provided to support that training.

Observation 7

The community colleges that have effectively engaged in community-based programming have established environmental scanning committees and have engaged those committees in study and analysis of their service-area communities to keep the college well informed about the major issues that are currently having a negative impact on the community and its people. Further, the committee has ranked the major issues in terms of their severity. The membership of these environmental scanning committees has included knowledgeable community leaders who have an interest in the welfare of the community and who can contribute the time needed to engage in a continuous study of the community. These environmental scanning committees have been trained by the community college's community-based programming management team, which also provides technical assistance to the committee in the collection and analysis of data about the community. In addition, the management team focused on teaching the environmental scanning committee group process skills and served as a facilitator to help the environmental scanning committee use those skills effectively.

Recommendation

The community college should establish, train, and use an environmental scanning committee to study and analyze the community in order to identify and rank the major issues that are affecting the quality of life of the residents of the community. The community college must extend every effort to ensure that the membership of the environmental scanning committee is representative and highly knowledgeable about the community.

Observation 8

Community colleges that have achieved the greatest success in community-based programming have involved their governing boards and other community leaders in evaluating and sanctioning the issues defined by their environmental scanning committee. The presidents of these community colleges have been mindful of the need to keep their college's governing boards involved in and informed about the college's community-based programming initiative. Further, these presidents have made sure that the issues identified have the total support of their college's governing boards.

Recommendation

The community college's president should seek and obtain the approval and sanction of its governing board and other community leaders on the importance of the issues identified by the environmental scanning committee and on the appropriateness of the college's involvement in resolving each of the issues.

Observation 9

To begin involving their community in resolving the sanctioned and approved issues, the community colleges that have been most successful in their community-based programming efforts have selected *one* issue for their initial community-based programming activities, rather than beginning work on a number of issues. This approach has enabled the community college to concentrate and focus its efforts, thereby acquiring experience and skills that will be valuable in dealing with future issues.

Recommendation

The community college should select one issue to begin its work in its service-area community. The issue selected should be one in which success can be achieved in resolving the issue or in which positive movement can be made toward resolution.

Observation 10

Community colleges that carefully studied, analyzed, and mapped both the target public affected by the issue and the stakeholders and that also involved the leaders of these groups in intensive dialogue about the issue, its importance, and the strategies for resolving it experienced the greatest success in community-based programming. Community colleges that placed little or no emphasis on seeking out and involving their target publics and stakeholders in relating to the issue and assuming a major role in resolving it experienced considerable frustration and difficulty in their efforts to obtain community involvement. Until the target publics and stakeholders affected by the issue become a party to resolving the issue and become actively involved, little or no success can be achieved.

Recommendation

The community college, through its community-based programming management team, should gain a thorough understanding of the target public and stakeholders who have an interest in seeing the issue resolved. Further, the community college's management team should identify the leaders of the target public and spokespersons for the stakeholder groups and engage these leaders in dialogue about the issue, thereby obtaining their support in working toward resolution of the issue. It is in this context that the leaders of the two groups agree to become a part of a coalition that will focus its attention and resources on resolving the issue.

Observation 11

Those community colleges that have experienced the greatest success in working with issue-specific coalitions have provided the coalition with technical assistance in acquiring a thorough understanding of the issue and reaching consensus about it as well as selecting the strategies needed to resolve the issue. In its work with the issue-specific coalition, the successful community college has functioned in a facilitative role and has not usurped the work of the coalition. These colleges have adhered closely to the principle that the coalition has the primary responsibility for resolving the issue and that the role of the community college is to assist the coalition in carrying out that responsibility. The issue can be resolved only by the coalition, not the community college, since the coalition is composed of leaders of those people who are affected by the issue and who must undergo change to resolve the issue.

Recommendation

The community college, through its community-based programming management team, should provide the coalition with the technical assistance and support to enable it to engage in actions leading to the resolution of the issue. This assistance should not be provided to the coalition in a manner that leads its members to believe the community college has the sole responsibility for resolving the issue.

Observation 12

Those community colleges that have been most effective in assisting their coalitions in resolving issues have provided the coalitions with technical assistance in translating decisions made by the coalition into a functional plan of action. These plans of action have been carefully designed to serve as detailed blueprints to guide the efforts of the coalition in resolving the issue. The plans of action define what actions are to be pursued, establish a schedule for the actions, identify the resources needed, and specify who will be responsible for providing those resources.

Recommendation

The coalition, with the assistance of the community-based programming management team, should design and develop a plan of action that will guide its efforts to resolve the issue.

Observation 13

Community colleges that have been the most effective have encouraged, monitored, and guided their coalition's implementation of its plans of action. The coalition's acceptance of primary responsibility for implementation of the plan of action is critical to its complete and successful implementation.

Recommendation

The community college should assist and guide the coalition in implementing the plan of action and should provide opportunities for the coalition to monitor and evaluate the effectiveness of its efforts.

Observation 14

The coalitions that have made considerable progress in resolving their respective issues have kept their attention and the plan's actions focused sharply on that process. The outcomes sought by the coalition have been carefully defined. Throughout the implementation of their plans of action, the coalitions have given careful attention to monitoring and evaluating the effectiveness of their efforts in moving toward resolution of the issue. Further, those coalitions that have succeeded in moving toward issue resolution developed and implemented evaluation plans that included a clear statement of (1) the outcome being sought, (2) the indicators that would show when the outcome had been attained, and (3) the appropriate methods for collecting the information needed to conclude that the issue had been resolved or that positive movement toward resolution had been made.

Recommendation

The community college, through its management team, needs to provide the coalition with technical assistance in defining and measuring the outcome sought. Further, the community college needs to help the coalition develop and implement an evaluation plan and interpret the results of the evaluation.

Observation 15

Those coalitions that have experienced the greatest amount of success in resolving their respective issues have made a concerted effort to keep their target publics, stakeholders, and other significant leaders and community groups informed about coalition efforts.

Recommendation

The community college's management team should assist the coalition in developing and implementing the appropriate means for reporting to and being accountable to stakeholders on the progress made and results attained in resolving its defined issue. In addition, the mass media and other communication channels should be kept informed throughout the implementation of the community-based programming process.

Observation 16

Because of the scope and complex nature of the issues being pursued by ACCLAIM's pilot colleges and their respective coalitions, their initial efforts have not resulted in total resolution of the issues. Nevertheless, positive movement has been attained. Using the results attained and lessons learned from these initial efforts, these coalitions have initiated a second planning cycle that focuses on further efforts to resolve their defined issues. While most of the coalitions have kept their original form, some have added new members.

Recommendation

The community college should help the coalition review the progress made in resolving the issue in its initial effort, identify obstacles encountered, and carefully document the lessons learned. Further, the coalition should be assisted in interpreting outcomes achieved and in applying the lessons learned to its second effort to develop a plan for further resolution of the issue.

Conclusion

This is a practical book intended to elaborate on the practice of community-based programming in the field. It is not a textbook, nor is it intended for the exclusive use of community college educators. It has applicability to all adult education organizations that have an interest in and commitment to resolving issues and empowering people. This book, then, is intended for pragmatic use by community college administrators, governing boards, and other influential community leaders interested in strengthening their community colleges, developing their communities, and serving the ends of democracy. We have dedicated our efforts to such leaders, and we commit our findings as tools to supplement their resourcefulness.

To these leaders, we say that our society today—and the issues that it now confronts and will likely soon face—demand that opportunities be provided for its leaders to become empowered to cope with and resolve these issues with minimal outside support. To strengthen this society and to empower its leaders, the community college must reposition itself to take a leading role in helping to resolve those issues that threaten our society.

Above all, we share with these leaders the time-honored knowledge that substantive change can best be made permanent by working *with* the people, not just *for* them. If you are one of these leaders, if you embrace aspects of what you find herein to inform your efforts as an agent for change, just remember that the basic principles of participation, collaboration, and communication are at the heart of this process: *The success of community-based programming depends upon commitment to the collaborative process.*

The community college is in the right place at the right time. More than any other public agency, more than any other educational institution, the community college has the opportunity, obligation, and resources to resolve the problem of disconnectedness in our society. As we look into the future, it *will not* be business as usual. It *should* be Participation + Communication = Collaboration!

About the Authors

Edgar J. Boone is Director of the Academy for Community College Leadership Advancement, Innovation, and Modeling (ACCLAIM) and is the William Dallas Herring Distinguished Professor in the Department of Adult and Community College Education at North Carolina State University. Prior to becoming Director of ACCLAIM, he founded and served for 28 years as Head of the Department of Adult and Community College Education at North Carolina State University. He has authored a number of books and articles on the programming process in Adult Education and the community-based programming process in the community college. He was inducted in the International Adult and Continuing Education Hall of Fame in 1996 and was the recipient of the USDA's Distinguished Leadership and Ruby Awards in 1989 and 1990.

George B. Vaughan is Professor of Higher Education, Associate Director of the Academy for Community College Leadership Advancement, Innovation, and Modeling (ACCLAIM), and Editor of the *Community College Review* in the Department of Adult and Community College Education at North Carolina State University. Prior to becoming a professor, he served as a community college president for 17 years. He has written a number of books and articles on the community college, including the *Community College Presidency.* He received the 1996 Leadership Award from the American Association of Community Colleges.

Rosemary Gillett-Karam is Associate Professor in Adult and Community College Education at North Carolina State University. Her research areas include community college leadership, women in higher education, and equity in higher education at NCSU. She is associate editor of the *Community College Review.*

Wynetta Y. Lee is Assistant Director for Evaluation of ACCLAIM and Assistant Professor in the Department of Adult and Community College Education at North Carolina State University. In addition to 10 years experience in program assessment/evaluation, she has extensive experience in program development and implementation in both higher education and non-profit organizations.

Brian Nichol is Visiting Associate Professor in the Department of Adult and Community College Education at North Carolina State University. He is a management teacher and researcher in the field of organizational behavior. As a consultant to ACCLAIM, he is working with colleges in the United States and the United Kingdom.

John M. Pettitt is Continuing Education Coordinator of ACCLAIM and is Visiting Assistant Professor in the Department of Adult and Community College Education at North Carolina State University.

Jacquelyn W. McCelland is Associate Professor in Family and Consumer Sciences at North Carolina State University and a Food and Nutrition Specialist with the North Carolina Cooperative Extension Service. She is the co-chair of the Nutrition and Wellness State Major Program and a member of the Scientific Board of the Institute of Nutrition of the University of North Carolina. Her publications focus on the roles of diet and nutrition in health and chronic disease.

Robert A. Rubin is Professor in the Department of Biological and Agricultural Engineering at North Carolina State University. He is an international authority on water and waste management. His publications focus on water quality, waste management, and other environmental issues.